God Is a Gift

God Is a Gift

Learning to Live in Grace

Doug Reed

THORNCROWN PRESS
EUREKA SPRINGS, ARKANSAS

Cover art courtesy of Jody Stephenson, Studio 62, Eureka Springs, Arkansas.

1st printing 2012 • 2nd printing 2014

ISBN 978-0-9846431-4-1
LCCN 2011927401

ATTENTION CORPORATIONS, UNIVERSITIES, COLLEGES, AND PROFESSIONAL ORGANIZATIONS: Quantity discounts are available on bulk purchases of this book for educational and gift purposes, and as premiums for increasing magazine subscriptions or renewals. Special books or book excerpts can also be created to fit specific needs. For more information, please contact doug@godisagift.com or call 479-253-7401.

To Ann, who loves me
and has been one of God's greatest gifts
in my life

Contents

Introduction

This is a book about relationship with God.

Jesus said that the greatest commandment is to love God—"You shall love the Lord your God with all your heart, with all your soul, and with all your mind."[1] And we might think the way we accomplish this is to become someone God could love; we believe that if we become what God wants us to be then God will become what we want Him to be.

Yet the New Testament presents a vastly different way of coming to love God. It begins not with doing or becoming but with *knowing*. It presents the revolutionary idea that the way to change our lives is to change what we think about God. (The scriptures call such an experience "a revelation.") Consequently, the mature Christian is not someone who has learned to behave properly but one who has come to know God.

If anyone ever demonstrated this way of thinking about God, it was Jesus. Many believed He loved people who God was not supposed to love, and He blessed people God was supposed to curse. Those who thought they were doing the best job obeying God often became His enemies. This irony alone should cause us to rethink the heart of God.

In my own life, growth always comes when I find out God is not who I thought He was. Every glimpse of Him relieves my fears of not measuring up. When I see more clearly who He is, I can also see I am someone God loves relentlessly. I am someone God wants around, which makes me want God around all the more. This vision also changes what I see when I look at my neighbor. He carries the title "beloved," too.

In this book, I hope to provide a little glimpse of what God wants for and from us. When the events of our lives seem like a mystery, it is often because we do not understand what God is trying to give us or what He wants us to give Him. By knowing these things—this relationship with Him—we can know peace.

We might think it an impossible task to know the Lord. He seems so mysterious and otherworldly—how can *anyone* grasp the infinite? Yet the scriptures often describe God with amazing simplicity. John reduced the essence of God to just three words: "God is love."[2] And I will provide four words to help us live in the meaning of John's proclamation: "God is a gift."

There are two ways we can approach our relationship with the Lord. One is the way of religion; it says our nearness to God is our accomplishment. The second is the way of grace; on this path our closeness to God is Christ's accomplishment. The former focuses first on doing and becoming; the latter focuses first on believing and being. Paul used the words "law" and "grace" to describe these two contrary ways of seeking God.[3]

One of the most important settings of the New Testament was covenantal transition; the old covenant was passing away and the new covenant was coming into fulness. We might view the conflicts of the first century as ones between good and evil, believing God was coming against the bad people and blessing the good. Yet if these are our thoughts, the Gospels become very confusing. Christ should have been the Pharisees' best friend and the tax collector's worst enemy. However, the opposite was true.

A better way to define the conflicts both Jesus and Paul faced is through the covenantal context. Those of the old system, in which people had to be worthy of God, were persecuting the people of the gift. As grace swallowed up and transformed all things, there were those who tried to stand in its way.

Our journey is not quite the same as that of our first-century brethren. We are not like the Jews who were steeped in Torah and the righteousness of the Law. Nor do we face the same temptations as the first-century Gentiles, or non-Jews. If someone came to us saying that salvation required circumcision, we would probably be astonished that a person could believe such a thing. Yet such thoughts were very powerful in the day of the apostles.

Though our circumstances are different, our journey is similar. The greatest struggle of the Christian life is not to change our bad deeds to good deeds. In fact, if this is our focus, we may find ourselves fighting God as the Pharisees of old. Our greatest conflicts with God are still over His gift, but understanding this struggle helps us make sense of God's dealings in our lives. He is working not so much to get us to stop doing bad things as He is to get us to embrace His grace and live in it. It is His gift that transforms us into His image.

When God's presence and blessing are things we earn, it opens the door for fear and a judgmental heart. The more we think our deeds are the measures of God's favor, the more we end up alone. We can always find a reason for God to reject our neighbor, and if we think God separates Himself from our neighbor, we will separate ourselves from our neighbor. Not only that, we will have trouble accepting ourselves. Those who seek to be worthy of God end up either in self-exaltation, self-loathing, or some combination of both.

Understanding that God is a gift transforms all of our relationships. It opens the door for us to love our neighbor *and* ourselves; if God embraces our neighbor, so must we. Since God has given Himself to us, we can no longer look at who we are or what we have done to measure our worth. Our worth is now tied to who Jesus is and what He has done. There are no longer any outcasts. By giving Himself, God has raised the worth of even the worst sinner to the heavens.

This book is the story of how God's gift lovingly conquered me. It comes from my thirty years of seeking the Lord as both a congregant and then the minister at world-renowned Thorncrown Chapel in Eureka Springs, Arkansas (there is more on this beautiful site on page 219). I do not share too many personal experiences, talking instead about many of Jesus's parables and other stories from the Bible. These accounts are not just about people who lived long ago; they are our stories, too. For example, one of Jesus's great parables is one we call the story of the prodigal son—a timeless tale of two brothers who had relationship problems with their father. I have been both of these fellows: the brother who ran from his father, thinking he could find something better, and the self-righteous older brother who was left isolated from his brother and his father. Yet as the father in Jesus's story loved both of his sons, God has loved me.

Coming to know God is the journey of a lifetime, and my prayer is that this book will help us take a few steps along the way. Thousands of years ago, a man named Moses prayed what seemed like an incredibly brash prayer. He asked to see God. The Lord put Moses in the cleft of a rock and allowed his servant to see only part of His glory.[4]

Let us all pray with such boldness. Let us ask not just for God's blessings; let us ask *for God*. When we do, we will find that our prayer is in no way presumptuous; rather, it is a reflection of the heart of God.

When the Lord answers, we probably will not see anything with our eyes; He will show himself to our hearts. But what the heart can see is far more beautiful and glorious than what the eye beholds. We will come to know that God is closer and more intimate than we could ever have imagined. We will see that He is always there, even when we think He is not. He is always giving us His gift even when He is taking things from our lives.

This vision of God's gift can transform our world today the same way it did in Jesus's time. We can come to understand how God changed everything in Christ, for He did not just forgive us and leave us with a promise of heaven. He came to make our lives *His* dwelling. He came to make the infinite and the finite one.

Therefore, I can think of no better way to begin this book than with Moses's prayer to the Lord: "Please, show me Your glory!"

— 1 —

From the Beginning

Genesis is a book of foundations that answers fundamental questions. Some people see the creation story only as the account of how God created the universe, established the Earth, and formed His most cherished creation, the human being. Of course, the details of how God did these things are a matter of hot debate. Were the six days of creation literal days? Is the Earth young or old? Is the theory of evolution the truth, a lie, or something in-between?

How we got here is an important issue, but it is not the only idea the creation story addresses. The story also helps us understand why we are here. Our view of how God made us has little impact on how we live our lives, but our understanding of *why* He made us will affect our entire outlook on life.

Not all of us will answer the how of creation, but we will all answer the why of creation. We probably will not answer this second question with profound words like a theologian or a philosopher. We might not even answer it consciously, but we will answer it in how we relate to God and to each other.

The writer of Genesis may have explained exactly how God made everything, but this was certainly not his greatest concern. The Genesis narrative is about relationship with God. It reveals what God wants *for* us and what God wants *from* us. These issues are at the heart of the creation story, and they will be at the heart of this book.

The Bible does not give much of a description of the Garden of Eden other than the fact that the Lord planted it and it was a place of abundance; Adam and Eve had everything they needed there. We might visualize a place of unimaginable beauty where there was no disease, no pain, no want, only bliss. Whoever imagines the Garden of Eden usually pictures his or her idea of a perfect world.

Obviously, if God were to create such a place, He must love us dearly. However, did God's love find full expression in the gift of the Garden, or did He want something more for us? Jesus said that He came that we might have abundant life.[1] According to some, this means God desires us to have an Eden-like existence: if we believe the right things and do the right things, we can have a good life approximating what God intended from the start. We can have everything we want, and we can rid our lives of the things we do not want. All we have to do is get in line with God's will. After all, God loves us and He wants to be happy, right?

It is true that Jesus came that we might know true joy. However, if we read the Gospels, we will see that Jesus's recipe for happiness does not include a trouble-free life filled with our every desire.

In the time of Christ, Palestine was under Roman occupation. When the Romans came, they brought unbearably high taxes, unimagined brutality, and Caesar worship, and most thought the Messiah would deal with these oppressors. He would come with a sword in His hand, crush the Gentiles, fill His people's bellies with milk and honey, and make things the way they were "supposed" to be. Israel would once again be the head and not the tail.[2]

Yet Jesus came with an unexpected definition of "the good life." He did not offer His people a perfect world; the gift He came to give was Himself. In John's Gospel, we see that Christ is the way, the truth, and the life.[3] To possess Him was to have abundant life, and only *perfect love*—not violence—would transform Israel's world into a beautiful place. Jesus came not to destroy the Romans but to change the Gentiles from enemies to brethren.

Ironically, those with the most imperfect world—the worst sinners, the weakest, and the poorest—often saw the kingdom of God most clearly. They were the first heirs to God's great gift; they were the first to behold perfect love. What Christ came to fix was the human heart. He revealed that Eden is far more a place inside us than a place we can see with our eyes. The Lord redefined who was rich and who was righteous. He became the measure of humanity's worth. Those who possessed Christ truly had it all: His new definition—His new *seeing*—changed everything.

To God, Christ is a far more important possession than a trouble-free life. Consider the Apostle Paul's mysterious thorn in the flesh.

And lest I should be exalted above measure by the abundance of the revelations, a thorn in the flesh was given to me, a messenger of Satan to buffet me, lest I be exalted above measure. Concerning this thing I pleaded with the Lord three times that it might depart from me. And He said to me, "My grace is sufficient for you, for My strength is made perfect in weakness." (2 CORINTHIANS 12:7–9)

What did Paul want God to remove from his life so badly? Some take the "flesh" in Paul's "thorn in the flesh" very literally. They say the apostle had an eye ailment or another physical problem. However, we can solve this mystery if we put Paul's words in the context of his letter to the Corinthians. Paul's thorn in the flesh was trouble; it followed him everywhere he went.

From the Jews five times I received forty stripes minus one. Three times I was beaten with rods; once I was stoned; three times I was shipwrecked; a night and a day I have been in the deep; in journeys often, in perils of waters, in perils of robbers, in perils of my own countrymen, in perils of the Gentiles, in perils in the city, in perils in the wilderness, in perils in the sea, in perils among false brethren; in weariness and toil, in sleeplessness often, in hunger and thirst, in fastings often, in cold and nakedness—besides the other things, what comes upon me daily: my deep concern for all the churches. (2 CORINTHIANS 11:24–28)

No one knew more pain, suffering, and plain old bad luck more than Paul. The Jewish authorities gave Paul the sentence of thirty-nine lashes five times, and the Romans beat him with rods three times;[4] his enemies tried to silence him with stones, rods, and whips. We might think that the apostle had divine protection while traveling for God, but three times his ship did not make it to port. Finally, Paul asked the Lord for a life that was less troublesome, to which God replied, "No!"[5] Obviously, God's great purpose for Paul was not a comfortable life. In fact, the Lord gave His servant a life that was unbearable at times. We must conclude that God's gift was so great that Paul's suffering was worth it. Yet what could possibly be worth such a price? Paul tells us in his letter to the Philippians: "I have suffered the loss of all things and count them as rubbish, that I may gain Christ...."[6]

We may wonder why God created humanity *knowing* we would fall. He, in fact, put the means of our failure in the Garden; He knew all the suffering that would follow Adam and Eve's sin. It must be that He had an end in mind far greater than the delights of the Garden of Eden. As it was with Paul, our loss led to a much greater gain: our destiny was not a perfect world but the perfect love of our Creator.

Some say God had a wonderful plan for us but we ruined everything, and we are left with this rotten place to live. God is far too perfect to be stuck with plan B, however. This flawed world was part of His plan all along. Its design leads to a new definition of the perfect world—one found *not* in the creation but *in Christ.*

The Garden was beautiful, but humanity could never find its destiny in the Garden alone. The beauty and abundance of Eden was merely a reflection of a greater gift, as created things can never complete a human being. Though the finite creation was marvelous, God intended humanity to find completeness in the infinite—His presence—on Earth.

If the only thing we hear from the creation narrative is that God wants to bless us with things, we have not heard the whole story.

The message of Genesis is that God wants *a relationship* with us; the story of Adam and Eve is about how humanity lost relationship with the Lord. The rest of the Bible is the story of how God gave it back.

The first thing God gave Adam was the blessing of the Garden; the second thing He gave was a command.

> *And the Lord God commanded the man, saying, "Of every tree of the garden you may freely eat; but of the tree of the knowledge of good and evil you shall not eat, for in the day that you eat of it you shall surely die." (GENESIS 2:16–17)*

This command might lead us to believe that what God wanted most from humanity was good behavior. He wanted us to be blameless in our deeds so we could stand before Him without shame. To achieve this obedience, God provided the opportunity for disobedience through the forbidden tree in the midst of the Garden. In this line of thinking, the Tree of the Knowledge of Good and Evil was humanity's great test—and we failed. God was angry, but He had mercy and sent His Son to save us. Even after Christ's work, however, we are still miserable sinners who cannot seem to please Him. From this viewpoint, God's message is still "You had better behave...or else!"

On the other hand, perhaps our fall was part of the Lord's purpose. Maybe God never intended for us to stand before Him on our own merit. It is possible that our failure was part of God's plan to lead us to the Tree of Life.

Consider these two ways of explaining human weakness. One perspective thinks God despises our shortcomings; He once called His creation "good," but not anymore. We turn our weakness into something very bad, sometimes even blaming God for our condition because we think He is the one who really made a mess of things. After all, He could have created us with enough backbone to say no to the forbidden fruit, right? The other perspective quite simply thinks our weakness is part of humanity's journey to God.

The difference between these two views is the difference between isolation and union. A perfect human being has no need for grace;

if he has enough merit, he can stand before God without Christ. However, he stands alone. Good behavior is the basis of his walk with God rather than oneness with Christ.

Weakness and failure are wondrous facilitators of union with Christ. We discover the meaning of grace and unconditional love *only* in lacking. A person who is not worthy can find his worth in Christ. A person who has no hope of walking with God alone must walk together with Christ. God wants our shortcomings to lead us somewhere—to Christ, not to self-loathing.

Furthermore, if perfect behavior is God's standard, we will be isolated from our neighbor as well. Suppose our neighbor is not "as perfect" as we are. Suddenly, we divide humanity between "us" and "them," those God loves and those God hates. We have heard the expression "God loves you and so do I." The expression "God hates you and so do I" is just as ingrained in humanity's psyche. History is replete with examples. Consider the 9/11 attack on the World Trade Center. What could justify such evil? The answer is simple. Those responsible thought someone did not measure up.

If our thought is that good behavior is God's highest goal for humanity, Jesus becomes a huge contradiction. One of Jesus's greatest opponents was the Pharisees. The average Pharisee fasted two days a week and paid his tithes to the penny.[7] If these very religious fellows were such good men, why does the Bible paint them as being so evil? If God values good behavior above all else, Jesus should have been the Pharisees' best friend. Instead, he befriended the worst sinners, such as the tax collectors and prostitutes—the very people God was supposed to hate. Obviously, we cannot contain the essence of the kingdom of God in humanity's idea of "good and evil."

God never intended for us to stand before Him alone. From the beginning, He wanted us to stand together with Christ—to *see* in the light of His perfect love. As troubling as it may sound, our weaknesses and failures are part of our journey toward union with Christ. God's ultimate definition of a perfect human being is not one who has never made any mistakes but one who has Christ. A commandment could never make a perfect human being. God never intended it, and neither should we.

Then the Lord God took the man and put him in the Garden of Eden to tend and keep it. (GENESIS 2:15)

After God blessed Adam and gave him boundaries, He put him to work. Adam tended God's Garden and named His animals. We might think God wanted someone to work for Him, and that was Adam's great purpose; serving the Lord is certainly one of the greatest and most noble pursuits in life. But is this the pinnacle of our purpose, or like God's finite blessings, is it part of something greater?

I have heard more than one devout Christian say that ministry is his or her life. Though this view is honorable, it has inherent problems. The Bible never defines ministry as life. The Gospel of John tells us that Christ alone is "the life." Too often we separate serving God from *relationship* with God. Before we can do for God, we must *know* God.

Ministry is partaking of the Lord. It is participating in His love for others. Consequently, our highest calling is to know the Lord and take part in who He is. When we fulfill our purpose, the doing follows.

People often ask me, "How big is your church?" Translation: "How important are you?" In twenty-seven years of preaching at Thorncrown Chapel, I have learned that my ministry is not what completes me, nor is it the measure of my worth.

When Christ died and rose from the grave, He became the sole measure of human worth. God's servants are supposed to help people find their worth in Christ—to illustrate in word and deed God's unconditional love. If our own worth becomes the size of our ministry, we are in danger of becoming facilitators of a system that is counter to God's gift; sometimes there is a fine line between working for ourselves and working for God. If we are not careful, padding church attendance can become an exercise in padding our own egos.

We must also realize that in the Garden of Eden there were no souls to save, no hurts to comfort, no hungry to feed, nor great missions to establish. At first, it was just Adam and God, and God did not need someone to work for Him; He could have tended the

Garden just fine without Adam's help. God *did* want something for humanity and from humanity, but the title of "servant" did not encompass His desires.

When God created Eve, humanity took a step closer to God's grand purpose.

> *And the Lord God said, "It is not good that man should be alone...."* (GENESIS 2:18)

If we are alone, our lives are miserable, no matter how many possessions we have. Our relationships make our lives complete. Yet this is an incomplete statement if it does not include God; *all* human relationships are interconnected. And we cannot separate relationship with God from relationship with each other.

John tells us in his First Epistle, "...everyone who loves is born of God and knows God."[8] He connects knowing God with loving one another. To John, knowing God is not just getting our facts straight about the Lord; it is *partaking* of God. In other words, loving is something we do not do alone. Loving our family, friends, and even our enemies is something we do together with the Lord. We participate in His love for our neighbor.

Jesus, in His teaching, gives us another perspective on how God has tied us to both Himself and to our neighbor: He connects loving our neighbor with loving God. It may sound strange, but we show God how much we love Him by loving our family, our friends, and our enemies. Likewise, if we hate our neighbor, we hate God. One of the wonders of creation is that our knowledge of God and our love for God are not complete without our neighbor, nor are our relationships with each other complete without God.

Therefore, when God created Eve, he was not just giving Adam a wife or helpmate. He was also giving Adam an avenue by which His beloved creation could have *more* of God.

All these things—God's material blessings, the life and work He calls us to, and the people He puts in our lives—are part of God's gift. However, none of them can adequately describe or contain God's desire alone; a higher purpose overshadows and encompasses each and every one. To fully understand what God wants, we must look past the creation to God Himself.

God is love. (1 JOHN 4:8)

When Moses stood before the burning bush and spoke with God, he asked what God's name was. The Lord's answer was *Yahweh* or in English, "I AM WHO I AM."[9] To the ancient Hebrews, a name was more than just an arbitrary title; it represented the essence or nature of the person who bore it.

Whenever God revealed more of who He was and what He was like, the Jews added to the name of God. For example, when Gideon was fearful, God gave him peace. Afterwards, Gideon built an altar to God and called it *Yahweh Shalom*, which translated to "the Lord is Peace."[10] Throughout the Old Testament, we see many such names of God, each revealing a little about who God is. In the New Testament, we see the revelation that surpasses and encompasses them all: "God is love."

Some say God has no needs; He is complete in and of Himself and could be perfectly happy if He were alone. From a certain perspective, this is true. However, if God is love, He does have one need: Love needs to give itself away. Love needs a beloved.

Theologians and philosophers have debated life's meaning for countless generations, sometimes concluding that our purpose is simply unknowable. However, the scriptures reveal a purpose so great that it compels worship. God wanted a creation He would not just bless or call to service, but one to whom He would give the greatest gift ever given—Himself. We were made to possess the gift *of God.*

This suggests a completely new definition of human completion— not one who "has it all" but one who has God. Likewise, a shameless human being is not one who has never done anything wrong but one who has Christ as the measure of his standing with God. The gift defines who we are; the gift makes us whole.

God's purpose also opens up new possibilities concerning the human condition. God created each one of us without hope of being good enough to stand before Him without shame. But our shame disappears when we see our solitude was never His intent. From the beginning, He wanted us to *stand together* with Christ. Our weaknesses and failures are our teachers; they lead us to grace.

God created us incomplete for good reason. We are each an empty cup that needs filling, and our yearning for completeness drives us to the gift. Like the prodigal son, we may stray, but our straying is part of our journey home. The gift is our destiny.

What God wants for us is Himself. And it cost God *everything*, even His own Son, to fulfill this desire. Yet, taking His gift is costly for us as well. The price we pay is not changing from a bad person to a good person; it is not becoming someone God could accept. We do not merely switch from the evil side of the Tree of the Knowledge of Good and Evil to the good side; we change trees altogether. We come to the Tree of Life. What we lose in this exchange is everything contrary to union with Christ, including our own righteousness.

Union is God's goal, and nothing less will satisfy Him or us. At the heart of creation is a love affair so extraordinary it surpasses our highest expectations.

— 2 —

The Two Trees

The Lord God planted a garden eastward in Eden, and there He put the man whom He had formed. And out of the ground the Lord God made every tree grow that is pleasant to the sight and good for food. The tree of life was also in the midst of the garden, and the tree of the knowledge of good and evil.
(GENESIS 2:8–9)

How we begin at "the beginning" is vital. The Tree of Life and the Tree of the Knowledge of Good and Evil have something to say about our relationship with God. They speak about salvation and the meaning of life, and how we define each of these trees will set the course of how we interpret the rest of the Bible.

Discerning the trees' meaning is not an easy task, but we have an advantage over the people of the Old Testament; we have the *whole* Bible. What began in mystery finds explanation in the New Testament. Therefore, when we look at the whole of scripture, these trees give up their secrets.

Understanding the Tree of Life hinges on our definition of the word "life." Many things come to mind when we ponder what it means to be alive. The most obvious is the state of our body. If we are breathing and our hearts are beating, we say we possess life.

Our lives are also the sum of who we are, what we have, the things we have done, and the things that have happened to us. If we have achieved or gained almost everything we want, we might say we have a good life. If we look at ourselves and we bear no resemblance to what we want to be, we feel dissatisfaction. If we have done little good for God or for our neighbor, we might even think we have wasted our life.

The scriptures present yet a third definition of life that most closely represents the nature of the Tree of Life, and it has nothing to do with our bodies or our experiences. In fact, we must look *away* from ourselves to find its essence. Christ is "the life."[1] We may still breathe, and we may be a good person with good possessions, yet in God's eyes, we are dead without Christ. It is only in the context of relationship with Christ that we live.

God's warning to Adam is confusing if we do not understand the way God defines being alive. On the day Adam partook of the Tree of the Knowledge of Good and Evil, the Lord said he would surely die. When the serpent spoke to Eve, however, he said the tree's fruit would not kill her.[2] Who was right? At first glance, it might seem the serpent was telling the truth. Adam and Eve's hearts did not stop the day they disobeyed, and they, in fact, lived long after that. The following years were hard but good.

But if we define life as God Himself, we see that Adam and Eve did die that day—they suffered *relational death*. This idea was very common in ancient Hebrew thinking. Paul talks about being dead in our trespasses and sins,[3] which has nothing to do with whether we are still breathing.

Jesus told the story of the prodigal son who left home for a life of sin. When the wayward son returned home, his ecstatic father exclaimed, "Bring out the best robe and put it on him, and put a ring on his hand and sandals on his feet. And bring the fatted calf here and kill it, and let us eat and be merry; for this my son was dead and is alive again; he was lost and is found."[4] Notice that the father said his son "was dead and is alive again," a notion that has nothing to do with biology.

When the Law came through Moses, God gave a vivid illustration of the death Adam suffered, and, amazingly, it was in the House of God. In the Hebrew Temple was the Holiest of Holies—an inner court surrounded by a thick veil. Beyond this covering was, in the Jewish mind, the place where heaven touched Earth. It was the most sacred space in the most sacred building in the world. If a worshipper could go beyond that veil, he would be in the presence of Yahweh, the God of Israel.

Embroidered on the veil was the image of angelic beings called cherubim.[5] They were not there to invite people in but to warn them to stay out. The Lord allowed no one to enter the Holiest of Holies save the High Priest of Israel, and he could only go beyond the veil one day a year.

When God banished Adam and Eve from the Garden, he placed cherubim and a flaming sword to guard the route to the Tree of Life.[6] What Adam and Eve lost at the fall was God, and *that* was their death. This spiritual death changed not only their relationship with the Lord, but also how they looked at themselves and how they related to their neighbor.

At this point, the theologians among us may protest, saying physical death is part of the curse God put on humanity. God said, "For dust you are, and to dust you shall return."[7] Even if biological death were part of the fall, the overwhelming focus of redemption is still restoration of relationship with God. John tells us in his Gospel that to have eternal life is to know Christ.[8] To God, eternal life is not a length of time but a person: he who has Christ has *the life*. Immortality is more about possessing the infinite God than about the state of our physical bodies.

To make the body the focus of redemption lessens God's gift or even redefines it. Many look forward to going to heaven someday. Having an immortal body that no longer suffers pain or sickness is not the best thing about heaven, however; it is that *God is there*. His presence is what makes heaven heavenly. Relationship with God is the heart of redemption.

Now the serpent was more cunning than any beast of the field [that] the Lord God had made. And he said to the woman, "Has God indeed said, 'You shall not eat of every tree of the garden'?"

And the woman said to the serpent, "We may eat the fruit of the trees of the garden; but of the fruit of the tree [that] is in the midst of the garden, God has said, 'You shall not eat it, nor shall you touch it, lest you die.'"

Then the serpent said to the woman, "You will not surely die. For God knows that in the day you eat of it your eyes will be opened, and you will be like God, knowing good and evil."

So when the woman saw that the tree was good for food, that it was pleasant to the eyes, and a tree desirable to make one wise, she took of its fruit and ate. She also gave to her husband with her, and he ate. (GENESIS 3:1–6)

From the beginning, God also set a forbidden tree in the midst of the Garden—the Tree of the Knowledge of Good and Evil. Some focus on the word "knowledge" in the tree's title, believing that, with God, ignorance really is bliss. From this perspective, knowing things is a threat to humanity's relationship with God, so He wants us to remain in the dark about how things really are. If we figure out how the Earth works, we will not need Him anymore.

There are a least two things wrong with this idea. First, it would make God the fraud and the serpent the purveyor of truth. If you read the rest of Genesis, you will see this is nowhere near the author's message. Furthermore, knowledge is no threat to God. The Bible is a book about relationship with the Lord. Nowhere does it present understanding—knowledge—as a problem.

Second, the name of this forbidden tree contains the words "good and evil." Its name is not "the Tree of Knowledge" nor is there any indication that the Tree of Life is the Tree of Ignorance.

Instead of analyzing the name of the Tree of the Knowledge of Good and Evil, it is helpful to ponder the mysterious serpent we presume is Satan. Learning his objective will help us discover why this terrible tree was so destructive.

If we watch TV or movies, we witness some strange ideas about the Devil. We have all seen scenarios where someone must make a decision. A little devil appears on one of their shoulders and a little angel on the other, and the two beings present their arguments. One tries to get the person to do bad and the other good, trading barbs until one wins. Many times, the devil comes out on top!

This representation gives the idea that God is all about being good and the Devil is all about being bad. If that were the case, however, the Tree of the Knowledge of Good and Evil would be a good thing. Partaking of it could help God's dearest creation learn the difference between God and Satan.

When Adam and Eve partook of the forbidden fruit, they did not suddenly figure out what was good behavior and what was bad behavior; they already had such knowledge. God told them what acceptable behavior was—it was very simple. Eating of the Tree of Life was good, and eating of the Tree of the Knowledge of Good and Evil was bad.

It is obvious that the serpent wanted Adam and Eve to disobey God, but he had an even more sinister objective: he wanted to steal the gift. He wanted to steal God from God's beloved, and he did so by offering a substitute, the Tree of the Knowledge of Good and Evil. Just as the Tree of Life embodied spiritual life, this wicked tree embodied spiritual death. Its essence was not just evil but *independence* from God. Its lure was the promise of fulfillment but in the creation rather than the Creator.

In this, we see the nature of Satan. His desire is not so much evil as it is disunion. His purpose is to keep us from finding our completion in the Lord. He is the master of broken relationship, and his weapon is deception.

Astonishingly, the Devil offered Eve *nothing* she did not already have. He tempted Eve by saying she would be "like God," but didn't God create her in His image? From the very beginning, God tied who Adam and Eve were to Himself. What the serpent did was break that tie. The Tree of the Knowledge of Good and Evil offered an identity separate from God.

When Eve partook of the forbidden fruit, she ripped the right to define who she was from the Lord's hands. This was the birth of self-definition or what the Bible calls self-righteousness. God defined Eve as good—He could do no less because her good came from Himself. Now, just as God was the source of His own righteousness, Eve had become the source of hers. Thus, in a perverted way, she had become like God.

From that point forward, she had to *earn* the title "good" and carry the label "evil" if she failed. The folly of her choice was that she now had to measure up to God Himself; the standard for humanity was God's righteousness. Yet God's righteousness was no longer a gift. We see the outcome in Paul's words, "...for all have sinned and fall short of the glory of God...."[9]

The serpent's desire was not solely that God's creation would become evil but that it would first become *completely separated* from God; evil would follow. When self is the measure of a person's righteousness, that person cannot know Christ as his righteousness. There can be no union. The gift is lost.

A second aspect of Eve's temptation came from Eve's own eyes. She saw that the Tree of the Knowledge of Good and Evil was "good for food, ...pleasant to the eyes, ...and desirable to make one wise" (Genesis 3:6). But what Eve saw in the tree is curious. She already had all the food that God supplied, she already saw the beauty of the Garden, and she knew the wisdom that comes from relationship with God.

What this second tree offered was *a replacement* for God. It promised to complete Adam and Eve instead of the Tree of Life. Humanity needed something to fill its empty cup, and the forbidden tree looked like a better choice than God. It was another lover, and that lover looked good.

Perhaps the Tree of the Knowledge of Good and Evil was more attractive than the Tree of Life. If not, maybe it could not have tempted Eve. She would have said, "I have the Tree of Life. Why would I need this obviously inferior tree?" Sin often appears more enticing than

God. Not only that, the wisdom of the forbidden tree seemed to be a better wisdom than the wisdom of God. Though the Lord gave Eve the visible finite creation, His wisdom was that the unseen, infinite God would complete her.

Living by the unseen takes faith, and the Tree of the Knowledge of Good and Evil had nothing to do with faith; it was all about seeing with the eyes. It appeared the finite creation could fulfill Eve better than God could, and there was no faith required. All she had to do was reach out and take what she wanted.

With the serpent's words we see the introduction of self-righteousness. And through Eve's own eyes comes the introduction of lust—the idea that getting what we see with our eyes completes us.

In an instant, the serpent had replaced God with self and the infinite with the finite. Union was broken, and death had come. The serpent had stolen the gift.

So when the woman saw that the tree was good for food, that it was pleasant to the eyes, and a tree desirable to make one wise, she took of its fruit and ate. She also gave to her husband with her, and he ate. Then the eyes of both of them were opened, and they knew that they were naked; and they sewed fig leaves together and made themselves coverings.

And they heard the sound of the Lord God walking in the garden in the cool of the day, and Adam and his wife hid themselves from the presence of the Lord God among the trees of the garden.

Then the Lord God called to Adam and said to him, "Where are you?"

So he said, "I heard Your voice in the garden, and I was afraid because I was naked; and I hid myself."

And He said, "Who told you that you were naked? Have you eaten from the tree of which I commanded you that you should not eat?"

Then the man said, "The woman whom You gave to be with me, she gave me of the tree, and I ate."

And the Lord God said to the woman, "What is this you have done?"

The woman said, "The serpent deceived me, and I ate."
(GENESIS 3:6–13)

God wanted to be the measure of Adam and Eve's acceptance and worth, not what they did or what they had. Worth and completion came from the Tree of Life—that direct tie God created between the finite and Himself. When this tie was broken, self became the new gauge of identity, and this exchange brought shame, fear, and a judgmental heart.

We have all felt shame. Perhaps something we did was exposed to others, or perhaps our humiliation was a private thing. It is hard to look people in the eye when we are ashamed because we feel our deeds have devalued us. We feel we are not worthy to stand in the presence of others, and we want to run and hide.

To avoid shame, we wear masks and tell lies to maintain our worth among our neighbors. In Adam and Eve's case, the one they compared themselves to was God, and they were sorely lacking. He was holy, and they were not. But there was no hiding from God.

It is easy to see how shame and fear go hand in hand; we *dread* rejection. Our need for acceptance is so strong, in fact, that at times we would rather die than do without it. Whenever acceptance is not a gift, there is the possibility of not measuring up, and with that possibility comes fear.

When Adam and Eve lost God as the measure of their worth, it affected not only their relationship with the Lord but also their relationship with each other. If one has to earn his or her own worth, comparisons follow. When who I am, what I have, or what I do is better than who you are, what you have, or what you have done, I can count you as unworthy. Devaluing you is a way to save or increase my own worth.

We see this in Adam and Eve's encounter with God. To preserve his own worth, Adam blamed Eve, and Eve tried to save herself by blaming the serpent. It was better to diminish someone else than to lose their own worth.

Adam and Eve were naked and unashamed before the fall. When they looked at themselves, they saw God's wonderful creation—something God Himself called "good." There was no need to cover that which was good, yet when they partook of the Tree of the Knowledge of Good and Evil, they suddenly saw something vastly different when they looked at themselves; they saw something they needed to hide. Their appearance had not changed, but their consciousness had.

The forbidden tree introduced a new consciousness to humanity. And it did more than open Adam and Eve's eyes to the fact they were naked. It exchanged God consciousness for self-consciousness, and consequently, sin consciousness.

This might sound like a complex concept to understand, but we have all experienced it; we have all done things that made us feel shame before God. And if our misdeeds are bad enough, when we approach the Lord, all we can see is our own unworthiness. We think God rubs our face in our own sinfulness with the hope that our shame will cause us to walk in a worthy manner. On the contrary, such thoughts are not New Testament thinking. Instead, Christ says "Look at me! Look at who I am and at what I have done for you on the cross." When we take our eyes off our own misdeeds and look at who Jesus is and what He has done, our shame flees. Sin consciousness disappears, and God consciousness takes its place. With *righteousness consciousness*, when we look at ourselves, we no longer see something of which we need to be ashamed; we see God's new creation—a creation that once again bears God's image. Only when we look at Christ do we see who we are, for through the cross our identity is forever tied to His.

The Tree of the Knowledge of Good and Evil exalted the finite over the infinite, bringing new ways of seeing that were not seeing at all but blindness. This tree contained the wisdom of the world. In partaking of it, Adam and Eve exchanged light for darkness and the truth for a lie. They lost the mind of Christ, and the reign of the mind of man began. Consequently, things like riches, beauty, power, importance, and righteousness gained new definitions centered on man rather than on God. Humanity now saw these things in a completely new way—a way that delivered not what the serpent promised but death.

What follows Genesis, chapter 3, is the story of redemption: God would raise up a people, and through those people would come a Messiah to save us all. Many look at this redemption as removing sin so humanity could be forgiven, but this is only part of it. Full redemption is the return of the gift of God. It is the end of disunion and the rebirth of union.

It is no wonder we see creation imagery and terminology so frequently in the New Testament. John begins his Gospel with wording similar to the Genesis, chapter 1, creation account, and Paul speaks of the birth of a new creation in Christ. It is no accident that the first book in the Bible begins with the loss of the Tree of Life and the Bible's last book, Revelation, ends with its return.

In the scriptures, we see how humanity wrestled with love and lost. But love's final triumph manifested in the person of Jesus Christ. He came to bring humanity back from the dead, to free us from the grip of darkness, and to bring us into the freedom of His marvelous light. The Bible is the story of a Creator who would not be denied. He created us for the gift, and in Christ, the gift triumphs over all.

The Return of the Gift

One of the greatest human needs is personal worth. We all want to be somebody important and we need people to value us. No one wants to be a nobody, and no one seeks titles such as "useless" or "no good."

The value others assign to us lifts our hearts to the heavens. The sound of applause is intoxicating. Words of praise are sweeter than honey. Yet a chorus of boos can deflate the human spirit in an instant. When others belittle us, it hurts more than any slap in the face.

Just as important—if not *more* so—is the worth we assign to ourselves. Others will always rate our value, but we also value or devalue ourselves. It is possible for our peers to pat us on the back constantly while we devalue their praise by constantly kicking ourselves for our shortcomings. We can also do the opposite, exalting ourselves for no good reason.

In the past, it was common for people to measure their worth by their heritage. This was especially true in the first century. God chose the descendants of Abraham to be His own, and that made them special. Of course, many thought this meant that all others were of less value; the further a person's family tree was from Abraham's, the more worthless he was. And because some Jews had "polluted" their heritage by marrying pagans, they had a hard time finding acceptance in the covenant community. The least of all were the Gentiles, a people so low the Jews called them "dogs." In first-century Palestine, there were two types of people, the circumcised and the uncircumcised, and the difference between the two was the difference between having worth and being worthless.

Our ancestry is not so much a measure of our value in our day. We tend to believe a person can rise above his bloodline and become somebody even if his father was "a nobody." To do such a thing in Christ's time might have been considered going against society if not God Himself.

But even if we, in our time, believe in a person's right to "rise above," we still have societal ways of measuring worth. We deem the guy who can score touchdowns more valuable than the fellow who fumbles the ball. The beauty queens get attention while "the ordinary" go unnoticed. The highly talented, intelligent, and creative get our adoration as the stars, but that leaves the majority of us in an "unimportant" void in-between.

Another way we gauge our importance is by what we have. Two people pull up in a parking lot. One is driving an expensive sports car and the other drives a car that barely makes it to its parking space. Which one of these fellows is "a somebody" and which is "a nobody"?

In the first century, many thought God favored the rich—and for good reason. The old covenant promised great prosperity to those who kept Torah, and the book of Deuteronomy lists the abundant blessings that would come upon those who obeyed God.[1] These people would be the first and not the last, the head and not the tail. They would possess health and wealth, and those who disobeyed would get quite the opposite. This mindset is perhaps why the disciples were astonished when Jesus said that it was hard for a rich man to enter the kingdom of God.[2] If a man who had earned the old covenant blessing could not enter in, who could?

This kind of reasoning was also common in the pagan world. Of course, the gods favored the rich—they were rich, were they not? If the gods liked you, they give you wealth and power. If they hated you, they made you poor and weak. And if the gods favored the upper class, this justified the rich oppressing the poor. It is amazing what we become capable of when we think God likes us better than someone else.

We judge each other by who we are and what we have, and the last great measure of human worth is what we do. In Jesus's day, there were those who kept Torah and those who did not. Some kept the Sabbath properly and worshipped correctly, keeping all the Jewish feasts and customs. Others failed to keep their obligations. There were those who kept themselves pure, not touching that which was unclean, and there were the unclean who were impure because of who they were or because of what they touched or ate.[3]

To be part of true Israel, a person had to be a descendant of Abraham, but he also had to keep Torah. Both were necessary to be part of the covenant community. Foreigners could find inclusion, but they never reached the status of true family.[4]

Those who deemed themselves worthy separated themselves from the unrighteous. Yahweh did not want lawbreakers in His presence, and what God rejects so must His people. Not only were the sinners not allowed to participate in the glorious Temple rituals, no one would associate with them in daily life. The righteous would not dine with them, stay in their homes, or even touch them for fear of becoming unclean.[5]

Such a fate was far more serious in the ancient Eastern culture than it would be in the modern Western culture. Back then, people were more corporate in their thinking; the individualism of the West is relatively new to humanity's consciousness.[6] A first-century Jew shared in the worth and identity of his community, and being shunned from Israel was like dying. The banned no longer lived and had no value.

In our modern culture, we still divide into "us" and "them" according to our deeds. There are those who are good at being good and those who are not, and one looks down upon the other. However, different groups have different definitions of being righteous. Our standards can be anything from going to church to recycling. We can always find a way to define ourselves as good and our neighbor as bad.

When Adam and Eve partook of the Tree of the Knowledge of Good and Evil, humanity tied its worth to self. We began to measure our value by who we are, what we do, and what we have. Fortunately, Jesus came to break that tie and restore the bond of human worth to God. He brought a completely new way of seeing our value—by looking at Him and not by looking at ourselves. He came to make human worth *a gift*, and in giving this gift, He not only restored relationship with God but He brought peace between us and our neighbor.

Jesus would finalize His gift at the cross, but it was already present in His life and ministry. Even the events at His birth foretold that God was about to turn the whole world upside down.[7] We marvel that God sent angels to announce the birth of the Messiah. Yet even more wondrous than their appearing was *to whom* they appeared. We might think the most important announcement ever given would come to the ones the world deemed most important. Perhaps the angelic beings would interrupt Caesar's day to tell him the true King of Kings had arrived. If not Caesar, at least they would wake up Herod, the king of Palestine. And if not him, certainly they would inform the religious leaders in Jerusalem.

The angels came to none of these, however. They came not to the greatest but to the least—the humble shepherds. In that day, shepherding was one of the lowliest professions on Earth. But God did not see unimportant people when He looked at shepherds. He saw people of great value and chose to announce to *them* that a ruler like no other had come, for this King would subvert the measures of the rich, the powerful, and the self-righteous and raise the value of even the lowliest to the heavens.

And when Jesus came to the place, He looked up and saw him, and said to him, "Zacchaeus, make haste and come down, for today I must stay at your house." (LUKE 19:5)

Sometimes we think God barely wants to be with us. Perhaps if we could do a little less of the things God does not like and do a little more of the things we know He likes, He would want to spend some time with us. After all, He is way up in heaven, and we have to coax Him down somehow, right?

Jesus wiped away such thoughts with the words "Zacchaeus, make haste and come down, for today I must stay at your house." Zacchaeus was a chief tax collector. If we made a list of the worst sinners in the United States, who would be at the top of our list? Without question, the tax collector would be at the top of everyone's list in first-century Palestine. Chief tax collectors did not fill out an application for their job; they paid for it. The Romans gave the position to the highest bidder. Tax collectors *bought* the right to cheat their own people.

Taxes hit the common man the hardest. People had to pay Rome but also King Herod. They paid tributes and direct taxes on land and duties and extra taxes on everyday items such as salt. There were no tax breaks for the poor or deductions for children. In fact, there was a head tax, which meant the bigger the family, the higher the taxes. In addition, Jews had to give tithes to build Herod's temple and support the priesthood.[8]

Some estimate that the total tax burden on the average family was 30 percent or more of the household's total income. This might not sound that bad when you add up all our modern taxes; most of us pay at least that. However, Palestine in Jesus's time was an agrarian society, and most citizens had only a fraction of the wealth we do today. Even without an excessive tax burden, a "good year" meant the average family could keep a roof over its head and all its stomachs full. In a bad year, the family had to sacrifice, maybe even go hungry part of the time. Add a 30 percent tax burden to a family that barely has the essentials already and you have a recipe for disaster.

Paying taxes was a matter of life and death. The Romans would sometimes destroy whole villages for being late with payments. The tax collectors themselves were little more than thugs. Rome gave them the power to do what was necessary to get Rome's money, including torturing not only men but also women and children.

The very rich offered "relief" for those who were behind on their payments, paying a debtor's taxes if he agreed to sign over the rights to his land and become an indentured servant. However, the land meant *everything* to the Jews. It was God's gift, a part of the Jewish identity, and its loss meant the debtor had failed both his family *and* his God.

The tax collectors were cogs in a machine that was squeezing the life out of the Jewish people, and it is no wonder everyone hated them. For some strange reason, we do not think it is as bad to rob a rich man as it is to rob a poor man. It is one thing to cheat a fellow who will not miss a little of his money, but to take a man's last morsel of food? That is low. And that is exactly what the tax collectors did. They were growing rich off the misery of the poor.

Perhaps Zacchaeus heard about the Rabbi Jesus, who actually *befriended* tax collectors. How could this be? Righteous Jews did not associate with sinners. Torah keepers were supposed to cast off evil men and isolate them from the faithful. Because people like Zacchaeus were an abomination to God, they were not allowed to worship in the Temple; they were unworthy of God's presence. But if Jesus was a rabbi like no other who embraced the wicked, this was something Zacchaeus had to see. He was short, so he climbed up in a tree to get the best possible view of the Lord.

Many onlookers probably wondered why Zacchaeus wanted to get close to Jesus: "What is this evil man doing up in that tree? Doesn't he know the Messiah will give sinners like him what they deserve?" Imagine the little tax collector's surprise when Jesus stopped, looked up, and called him by name. "Zacchaeus, make haste and come down, for today I must stay at your house!"

Zacchaeus deserved shame, but Jesus honored him. The Lord did not wait for this evil man to become worthy of God's presence; He gave God's presence as a gift. He simply announced that He was coming to stay with a man whose life was a mess.

No doubt, prior to this day, people threatened Zacchaeus countless times with the wrath of God. In the past, all the condemnation in the world could not penetrate this chief tax collector's seared conscience. Yet this hardened sinner had no defense against love. When Jesus gave honor instead of shame, it broke Zacchaeus's heart. Love conquered him, and he became love's willing slave.[9]

God's Law in the Old Testament required a man who cheated another to pay back what he stole plus 20 percent.[10] Tax collectors of the day commonly overcharged people and kept the difference for themselves. After Jesus blessed him, Zacchaeus proclaimed that he would pay back four times what he had stolen. And not only that, he would give half of all he had to the poor. Jesus answered by saying that the little tax collector was a son of Abraham.[11]

In Jesus's time, everyone had an opinion about who were the true sons of Abraham. The Pharisees thought they were worthy of this distinction because their lineage extended uninterrupted back to Abraham. And they were pure not only in their lineage but in their deeds. The Sadducees thought the same about themselves, but they had closer ties to the Temple. Surely, that made them God's favorites. A third group, the Essenes, believed the Jewish Temple was corrupt, so they isolated themselves on the northwest shore of the Dead Sea. In their mind, they were the true "Sons of Light," and when the Messiah came, He would do away with all the sinners and use their community to establish a new Israel.[12]

Everyone thought that only the most righteous got the title, "Son of Abraham," yet Jesus gave it to a tax collector. He responded to outrageous sin with outrageous love, not with judgment. This was a living illustration of the nature of the kingdom of God, and at its heart was the unconditional love of Christ. Jesus revealed infinite love in His ministry, and He finalized God's gift at the cross.

In the story of Zacchaeus, we see the human response to divine love, and that is to love in return. Some say that Zacchaeus became a son of Abraham when he changed his ways. However, the story clearly shows that God's grace came first, and grace turned a heart of stone into a heart that *belonged to God.* We see this pattern throughout the ministry of Jesus. He loved first without condition, and people responded by loving Him in return.

And when John had heard in prison about the works of Christ, he sent two of his disciples and said to Him, "Are You the Coming One, or do we look for another?"

Jesus answered and said to them, "Go and tell John the things [that] you hear and see: The blind see and the lame walk; the lepers are cleansed and the deaf hear; the dead

are raised up and the poor have the gospel preached to them. And blessed is he who is not offended because of Me."
(MATTHEW 11:2–6)

Jesus ended his answer to John's disciples with "blessed is he who is not offended because of Me." Why would healing the infirm or preaching the Gospel to the poor offend anyone? To answer this question, we must understand that Jesus's miracles were not just miracles; they were also statements about the nature of God's kingdom. Likewise, the way He treated the poor was also a revelation.

Many in that day thought the sick were God's rejects. In John, chapter 9, Jesus's disciples encountered a man born blind. They asked the Lord if it was his sin or the sin of his parents that caused the man's blindness. Most people believed those who had leprosy and those who could not walk, see, or hear were just getting what they deserved. This idea probably came directly from Torah, which says God will curse the disobedient and their children with infirmity.[13]

The Law of Moses said certain animals, people who were bleeding or wounded, dead bodies, and lepers were unclean. And that which God curses man also curses. Torah restricts the lame, blind, and deaf in temple worship, but in Jesus's day, the Pharisees included those with these physical afflictions among the unclean as well.[14] Not only the infirm but also certain sinners were on the "do not touch" list. Recall when Jesus dined with a Pharisee in Luke, chapter 7, and a woman who was a sinner washed Jesus's feet with her tears and wiped them with her hair. The Pharisee was appalled at the sight of a sinner touching a holy man.

The idea of clean and unclean permeated the lives of Torah-keeping Jews. Cleanliness was more than a matter of being sanitary; they believed unclean things were an abomination to Yahweh, and He would not tolerate them in His presence. If a person touched something unclean, he would become unclean and suffer the Lord's loathing. Then, to get right with God and the community, he would have to follow elaborate steps to become clean again. To the Jews, clean and unclean were more about relationship than germs.

And along came Jesus, who laid His hands on the sick to heal them. In our day, we view this as a technique, sometimes placing our hands on someone who is sick or hurting when we pray for them. We do this because this is what Jesus did. Yet when Jesus touched the infirm, it was far more than a method; it was a statement. He was touching someone you were not supposed to touch. The lame, the blind, and the lepers were unclean—*unworthy*. The Law said, "Become clean and God will touch you." Just the opposite, Christ touched people, and they became clean.[15]

Under the old covenant, God withdrew from what was unholy; under the coming kingdom, God embraced people who were unholy and made them holy. God was giving Himself as a gift without regard to who a person was or what that person had done. Cleanliness no longer came from not touching this or that or from washing correctly. It came from possessing the gift of God in Christ Jesus.

Imagine being lame, blind, deaf, or a leper in that day—you were God's "reject." If you were born blind or infirm, you bore the label "unclean" your entire life and you died with it; you had no hope of being pure. If you were a leper, you had to announce your presence by crying "Unclean!" Everywhere you went, you had to make it clear you were not only sick but unworthy of God and of all Torah-keeping Jews.

Then the Rabbi Jesus comes your way. You might think He would be merciful and heal you from a distance. After all, the good teacher would not touch what was unclean. Instead, He approaches you, and (you can hardly believe it!) He touches you. In an instant, your body is whole. But the Messiah has not only given you health, He has also given back your worth as a human being. There can be no doubt that you are God's beloved, not an abomination. Christ has healed your body *and* your soul.

The poor, in many respects, were in the same category as the infirm. In most people's minds, the poor, while not unclean, were still without God's favor. Today, we do not realize what an enigma Jesus was in this setting. No one had *ever* seen anyone like Him—someone who went *first* to the most unworthy and then chastised those who boasted in their personal worth.

There is only one thing that could turn the world upside down and make the first last and the last first: the arrival of the gift of worth in Christ Jesus. The gift gave infinite worth to the outcasts—to the finite—and shamed the proud.

In 63 BC, the conquering Roman general Pompey marched into Jerusalem. His first stop was the Jews' most sacred building, the Temple. He walked straight into the second court, which was forbidden to foreigners, marched up the steps leading to the third court, and then he, a pagan, entered the most forbidden place on Earth, the Holiest of Holies. There, he stood and laughed at Israel's God.[16] This was a harbinger of very hard times for God's chosen people, but the Romans were not the first to bring oppression to the people of Palestine. Ever since God's people returned from Babylonian captivity around 400 years earlier, things were not right in Israel. God's people were supposed to be the head and not the tail, the first and not the last. Except for a period of about 100 years after the end of the Maccabean Revolt in 165 BC, one Gentile nation after another dominated God's people. First there were the Babylonians, then the Persians, the Greeks, the Egyptians, and now the Romans.

When the Romans came, they brought their pagan gods with them. Philip, the son of Herod the Great, went so far as to build a temple for Caesar worship in Caesarea Philippi (formerly the city of Paneas). Roman taxes broke the back of the common man making many destitute. We have accounts of people resorting to eating grass and the bark of trees to survive. In the cities, multiple families often lived below the poverty level in cramped conditions on very small parcels of land.[17] The Romans enforced their will with an almost unimaginable brutality. Josephus, a first-century historian, wrote that the Romans crucified over 10,000 Jews in Jerusalem alone and countless thousands in the surrounding cites.[18]

The people needed a Messiah—a Savior/King—to deliver them. God sent their Savior, but he was not the kind of king they expected. The people looked to the past to form their image of a deliverer: the Messiah would be the Son of David. Whenever David had a Gentile problem, he picked up his sword and put the pagans in their place.

Just a few generations before the time of Christ, another Messiah figure, Judas Maccabaeus, appeared to rescue Israel from another blight of pagan oppression and defilement of the Temple. The Jews called him the "Hammer of God." Judas won what seemed to be a miraculous victory against great odds, and when he, their hero, entered Jerusalem, the people spread out palm branches as he rode past.[19] Almost 200 years later, they did the same thing for Jesus when He entered Jerusalem.

The Gospels reveal that many people expected Jesus to be their King, but no one expected that He would bring *forgiveness* to the Gentiles instead of destruction. He would come not to raise the Jew above the Gentile but to make the Jew and Gentile *brethren*. Such a work was so wondrous, so stunning, so unbelievable that many could not fathom it. Christ had come to *save* His enemies.

Early in His ministry, Jesus left His own people and went among the Gentiles to a place called the Gadarenes.[20] We know this place was Gentile territory because of its pig farmers; Jews did not mix with swine or Gentiles. Tombs were also off limits, but a graveyard in Gardarenes is *exactly* where Jesus was headed. There, living among the tombs, naked and totally insane, was a Gentile possessed by a legion of demons, and he looked more like a wild animal than a man. Jesus delivered this foreigner with a word and cast the demons into a nearby herd of pigs. A most unclean Gentile met the King of the Jews that day, and the King *loved* him clean through.

This was no chance encounter; the Lord did not just happen upon this man. Jesus went looking for this Gentile in the midst of uncleanness that would turn a Torah-keeping Jew's stomach. The Jews believed Gentiles could seek Yahweh, but they would have to embrace Torah and become clean first. Once they qualified, they could have access to the covenant community. The Lord did not wait for this fellow to repent and become clean. He did not even wait for an invitation. He went looking for the worst Gentile imaginable.

It is a great miracle that Jesus cast a legion of demons into a herd of pigs and delivered the man, but even more astonishing was what the miracle said: God was embracing the Gentiles. He, in fact, was going to look for them. What would this say to the disciples who witnessed the miracle? It would say grace has no limits—the gift of worth is for anybody. There are no qualifications. If God was giving favor to people He was supposed to destroy, the kingdom of God had come, and it was bigger than the disciples ever imagined.

Grace is God being where He is not supposed to be, accepting what He is not supposed to accept, and touching what He is not supposed to touch. God's great gift of worth in Christ Jesus brought a new way seeing God, our neighbor, and ourselves. It broke down the boundaries not only between God and humanity, but also between the rich and the poor, the somebodies and the nobodies, and even the righteous and the unrighteous. In Jesus's ministry and teaching, God had begun the work of summing up all things in Christ. God once again was giving the gift of Himself through Christ, and those who have God have *infinite* worth.

— 4 —

Participation in the Gift

Christ's unconditional love is a difficult concept to grasp from the human perspective. In fact, we can present many arguments against it: "If God is a gift, no one will serve God. And if we can't do anything to make God love us more, and we can't do anything to make Him love us less, we won't do anything good. We may even do evil, because what we do or do not do has no bearing on our relationship with God." These are common objections to the idea of grace, as many believe fear of rejection is a necessary ingredient in our walk with God. We must have the threat of punishment when we do wrong, and we need the promise of a big payoff for doing good.

Such ideas sound reasonable, but how true are they? For about 1500 years, old covenant Israel had a performance-based relationship with the Lord. When they obeyed, God blessed them, and when they disobeyed, God cursed them. Israel's history was a roller coaster ride. But if you have ever ridden a roller coaster, you know it always ends up going downhill, and such was old covenant Israel's fate. In spite of its great rewards and punishments, the system in which God's people had to earn their worth failed.

Jesus came to bring a new covenant in which He—not the self— would be the measure of human worth. Entering this new covenant required letting go of the old system, however. But for those who had the courage to make this exodus, their home became love instead of lawlessness. Grace transformed their relationship with God and with their brother. It did not free them to do evil; it freed them to love God and their neighbor.

If we study Jesus's teachings, we will quickly see that the gift of worth is not something we tuck away in our back pocket and then present to God in heaven after we die. The Lord's gift is the basis of the kingdom of God here on Earth; Christ's mercy and kindness is our foundation. Part of living in the gift is giving it to others, and we cannot fully experience God's grace without doing so.

Judge not, and you shall not be judged. Condemn not, and you shall not be condemned. Forgive, and you will be forgiven. Give, and it will be given to you: good measure, pressed down, shaken together, and running over will be put into your bosom. For with the same measure that you use, it will be measured back to you. (LUKE 6:37–38)

Some people love the above passage, while others think it must be a mistake—especially the part about not judging or condemning. The latter believe if we are not supposed to judge anything, then anything goes. We all agree that we need to be merciful, but how do we do this without dismissing the idea of right and wrong?

Here is where the context of this passage becomes important. If we read the words surrounding this text, we see that Jesus spoke of many things we should and should not do. It is ridiculous to think the kingdom of God has no standards. Yet Jesus's instructions do have a basis, and that basis is the gift of worth.

And whoever says to his brother, "Raca [mindless one]!" shall be in danger of the council. But whoever says, "You fool [godless one]!" shall be in danger of hellfire. (MATTHEW 5:22)

In this passage, Jesus talks about the sin of contempt, but why would looking down on a fellow human being be such a crime in God's eyes?[1] It is because it does such violence to the kingdom of

God. The more a crime is counter to the highest values of a society, the greater its consequences. At the core of the kingdom is God's tie to humanity. If Christ has become the measure of human worth, devaluing our brother becomes the epitome of blindness and an insult to Christ and the cross.

Jesus requires that we leave behind the old system where "we got what we deserved" for the new system of grace, where we get the *opposite* of what we deserve. We cannot hold two measures in our hand at the same time. If we believe the measure of our brother's worth is who he is or what he does, we will give ourselves the same measure. A judgmental or condemning heart does not negate grace; it blinds us to it. And if we cannot see grace for our brother, we cannot see it for ourselves.

Suppose our neighbor wrongs us, or maybe he is weak where we are strong. We could let go of the new measure of grace and once again pick up the old measure of self. Consequently, we would begin to build a case against our brother, becoming his judge by weighing his worth according to what he has done or not done. And while we may think we are raising God's Law as the standard, we are really raising *ourselves* as the standard. If our neighbor's crime was to diminish us, we diminish him, declaring him unworthy of God. Where self is the measure of worth, the way to raise or preserve our own worth is to devalue someone else. In a sense, a judgmental heart is about self-preservation. But if God's Law were really our criterion, it would condemn us, too.

When Jesus said not to judge, He was not saying there are no longer consequences for our brother's actions. Rather, He was warning us not to imprison our brother in the old system, for in doing so, we imprison ourselves. The moment we pick up the old measure of worth for our brother, we drop the new measure for ourselves. We cannot live in the old covenant and the new covenant at the same time.

One of the great ironies of the kingdom of God is that the way we preserve our own worth is by preserving our brother's—even if he has wronged us. Blessing those who seek to steal our worth keeps our own worth intact. Though they wrong us, we respond according to the grace in Christ, giving them the opposite of what they give us. Though they see us as valueless, we see their value as infinite in Christ. Though they take from us, we bless them. And when we do so, grace becomes our fortress and our worth, something *no one* can steal. In freeing our enemy, we free ourselves.

The things Jesus said not to do stem from a system where the measure of worth and blessing is Christ; we are not to condemn or judge. Jesus also provided a "to do" list that likewise stems from God's gift.

It is curious that two of God's "to do" instructions are to forgive and to give. "Forgive, and you will be forgiven. Give, and it will be given to you..." (Luke 6: 37–38). At first glance, it might appear that Jesus is putting us back under the system where we earn our standing with God. But does our giving turn the Lord into a giver? Does forgiving others make Him forgive us?

When we believe these things, we open ourselves to pride. If our deeds give us our place with God, they can give us a place above others. And many people have trouble receiving things they did not earn, because they think it somehow diminishes their worth. The giver, in their eyes, is above the receiver. Likewise, we can put the forgiver above the forgiven.

Christ never meant His kingdom teaching to lead to such conclusions. His sayings are not just commandments; they are a picture of a life connected to God. God is a giver *and* a forgiver. The Lord's great gift to us is Himself, and if God is our gift, so is a giving and forgiving heart. Therefore, when it comes to grace, having and doing go together. The more we have, the more we do. The more we do, the more we have.

Forgiving and giving increase our experience of God's kindness; they turn us into receivers. Forgiving another opens our eyes to how much God has forgiven us, and giving unmerited blessings removes the shackles of having to be worthy from the recipient as well as the giver. Those who bless others bless themselves. Jesus compares God's kingdom to a party or feast in several places in the Gospels.[2] Giving and forgiving are our way of joining the party, and the party is not just for us but for our neighbor—for all. Giving and forgiving do not change God; *they change us.*

Contrary to what we often hear, sometimes even at church, we are to be intercessors, not judges. An intercessor is one who is a channel of grace and mercy, whereas a judge is a conduit for condemnation and judgment. An intercessor is one who sees something about another that that person cannot see for himself. He sees the presence of the kingdom where others cannot see it, and he prays accordingly. Far too often, the church gives up the role of intercessor for the role of a judge. In doing so, the church blinds itself to the beauty of the kingdom of God. In seeking to trap another, it traps itself. The church is to give the gift of worth to the world, not take it away. And that is our task as individuals, too.

> *And the King will answer and say to them, "Assuredly, I say to you, inasmuch as you did it to one of the least of these My brethren, you did it to Me." (MATTHEW 25:40)*

I once heard someone say, "I love Jesus. I just can't stand His people." Really? I have no doubt this person had problems with God's people, but does he love Jesus? The scriptures tell us that Jesus and His people go together. To love one is to love the other, and to hate one is to hate the other. Likewise, to devalue one is to devalue the other.

Many today speak of how wonderful God is but in the next breath speak of how miserable His church is. This sentiment reveals where they live—in the system where worth comes from who they are and what they do rather than from Christ. Such a system separates the head from the body.[3] It's not a pretty picture, but in reality, this is what they have done.

Christ and His people are one. If we look upon His people and do not see the beauty of Christ, we have a seeing problem. Sometimes we think we can shame God's people into being what they are supposed to be, but shame is a product of a paradigm where worth is not a gift. The biblical way of changing God's people is for them to see their connection to Christ. Who He is makes them who they are, and to devalue them is to break that connection.

Seeing is very much a part of the kingdom of God. When Jesus looked upon the infirm, the sinners, and the Gentiles, He did not see God's outcasts; He saw God's beloved. If we cannot see what He saw, we cannot see the kingdom of God, for it is found in the faces of His people—even the least of them. If we cannot see the kingdom, we cannot change our world. It's the kingdom's presence that changes everything.

> *You have heard that it was said, "An eye for an eye and a tooth for a tooth." But I tell you not to resist an evil person. But whoever slaps you on your right cheek, turn the other to him also. If anyone wants to sue you and take away your tunic, let him have your cloak also. And whoever compels you to go one mile, go with him two. Give to him who asks you, and from him who wants to borrow from you do not turn away.*
>
> *You have heard that it was said, "You shall love your neighbor and hate your enemy." But I say to you, love your enemies, bless those who curse you, do good to those who hate you, and pray for those who spitefully use you and persecute you, that you may be sons of your Father in heaven; for He makes His sun rise on the evil and on the good, and sends rain on the just and on the unjust. For if you love those who love you, what reward have you? Do not even the tax collectors do the same? And if you greet your brethren only, what do you do more than others? Do not even the tax collectors do so? Therefore you shall be perfect, just as your Father in heaven is perfect.* (MATTHEW 5:38–48)

At this point, we might be thinking, "Wait a minute! It sounds like living in God's kingdom will turn us into a doormat. People will walk all over us if we bless those who wrong us." Worldly logic says that if we give, we will just end up broke, and if we do not hit back, we will just get beaten up a lot. But make no mistake. Jesus is talking about overcoming in this passage, and in the kingdom, we overcome evil with good.

When we put Jesus's words in their context, they become all the more extraordinary. Oppression and cruelty were the order of the day in first-century Palestine. If the Romans, with their soldiers and tax collectors, were not making life miserable, some other local ruler was. Many thought the solution was to fight violence with violence, and Jewish zealots believed God would honor them with victory if they took up the sword against Rome.[4] There were also men known as bandits, but they were more like Robin Hood, robbing from the rich and giving to the poor. Another resistance group was the Sicarii, or "Dagger Men," who would hide short knives underneath the layers of their clothing. At opportune times, they would strike against Roman sympathizers. Rome labeled all these rebels traitors and crucified them liberally.

To make matters worse, many false prophets and messiahs promised victory over Rome, often claiming the title "Savior/King." The Jews had a litmus test to decide who was telling the truth, however. If a would-be Messiah ended up on a Roman cross, he was a false prophet. It was unthinkable that God would allow the Romans to humiliate His anointed one.[5]

Into this chaotic world, Jesus came with His astonishing words. He said that when someone strikes you across the cheek, turn the other one. He was talking about Rome, because that was the way Roman soldiers treated people. He said that when someone made you carry their pack one mile, carry it two. This was also a reference to Rome, because a Roman soldier had the right to conscript anyone to carry his pack for one mile. Jesus said the way to deal with your enemies is to love them, forgive them, and even treat them with astounding generosity. In light of the turmoil of first-century Palestine, these words must have been troubling—they still are today. How can giving our enemies the opposite of what they give us be victory?

To God, if we become just like our enemies, they have beaten us. If someone says unkind things about us and we say unkind things in return, what is the difference between them and us? Their hatred has made us hateful and dragged us right back into the old system where worth is tied to self. In that old realm, people build up themselves by tearing down others.

When we place Jesus's advice to turn the other cheek in its cultural context, it's easier to understand. The ancient world was an honor- / shame-based culture.[6] Today, when we think of a backhand across the face, our first thought is "Ouch!" In the first-century world, however, the shame would be much more hurtful than the physical pain. If a Roman soldier stuck you across the face, he wanted to hurt you, but even more, he wanted to dishonor you.

If you turned the other cheek, almost asking him to slap you again, you would be proclaiming that he could not diminish your worth. Your honor would be attached to Christ, and no backhand can break that tie.

The old system, where worth came from self, gave strength to insults and hate. Christ took away that power. Consider Paul's words in Romans, chapter 8:

> *What then shall we say to these things? If God is for us, who can be against us? He who did not spare His own Son, but delivered Him up for us all, how shall He not with Him also freely give us all things? Who shall bring a charge against God's elect? It is God who justifies. Who is he who condemns? It is Christ who died, and furthermore is also risen, who is even at the right hand of God, who also makes intercession for us. Who shall separate us from the love of Christ? Shall tribulation, or distress, or persecution, or famine, or nakedness, or peril, or sword? As it is written:*
>
> *"For Your sake we are killed all day long;*
>
> *We are accounted as sheep for the slaughter."*
>
> *Yet in all these things we are more than conquerors through Him who loved us. For I am persuaded that neither death nor life, nor angels nor principalities nor powers, nor things present nor things to come, nor height nor depth, nor any other created thing, shall be able to separate us from the love of God which is in Christ Jesus our Lord.* (ROMANS 8:31–39)

Many call turning the other cheek being weak, but the early Christians called it reigning with Christ. It was living in a kingdom where their honor was untouchable.

Returning a good deed for a bad one furthers our triumph. Jesus said when a Roman soldier makes you carry his pack one mile, carry it two. The way you overcome in that situation is not to hate those who wrong you but to show stunning charity instead. God was giving the gift of worth in Christ, even to the soldier. Though your oppressor might be blind to your importance, you must not be blind to his. Your response, therefore, would be to treat your persecutor as a person of value, giving him a blessing rather than a curse, and loving him rather than hating him.

In a way, returning love for hate is an act of defiance. Such an encounter between a child of the kingdom and his opponent is a clash between two powers. In the old kingdom, we overcame evil with evil, but in the new, we must overcome evil with good. Imagine how a Roman soldier who received such kindness would feel. He might not drop his sword, but he would certainly be disarmed. He would have a hard time hating the one who served him—he might even feel ashamed.

Not too long ago, I was looking at two publications that are polar opposites on just about everything. One side wrote articles telling how terrible the other side was; in their opinion, God was obviously against their opponents. Then I looked at the other publication, and they said the same thing, even using the same adjectives to describe their rival. In fact, it was so similar that we could take an article from one, change the nouns, keep the same adjectives and descriptive phrases, and then use that same article in the opposing publication. I concluded that these people were actually *just like each other*, exchanging hate with hate, and they did not know it!

What if one publication were different? What if they began to write about how much God loved their opponent, and they gave a blessing in return for a curse?[7] What would happen? Such kindness would expose the darkness of the other side. The greater the love given in return for hatred, the more apparent the hatred becomes. If we respond to darkness with more darkness, evil can hide. Darkness is exposed with light, not more darkness.

We must not let those who wrong us steal the gift of worth from our hearts. If we withhold it from them, we once again imprison ourselves in the system where worth is earned. The way to be free is to forgive. Our acts of kindness may not change our enemies, but they will change *us*. They will open up our hearts to God's grace, and His love will become our dwelling. We will be free.

The gift of worth in Christ Jesus is subversive; there is no defense against love. Astonishingly, our relationship with God is strongly tied to our relationship with our enemies. While we may think our lives would be better off without those who offend us, our enemies can be our best teachers. Return love in the face of hate and victory reigns infinite in the kingdom.

What does God look like? Maybe we have dreamed of seeing Him face to face someday—would He look like us? Would He appear as a light so bright we cannot fathom it, or would He take some other form? Such thoughts are wondrous, but in the kingdom of God, "seeing" God has little to do with our eyes. We behold God when we forgive our neighbor or bless someone. We see Him even more clearly when that person does not deserve the blessing. When we do such things, we not only get a glimpse of God, we come to *know* Him.

The phrase "to err is human and to forgive is divine" also translates as "forgiveness is *participation* in the divine." When we pray to see God and our enemy shows up at our doorstep, we might first wonder *why*. Then God says, "You asked to see Me. *Look!*"

For the kingdom of heaven is like a landowner who went out early in the morning to hire laborers for his vineyard. Now when he had agreed with the laborers for a denarius a day, he sent them into his vineyard. And he went out about the third hour and saw others standing idle in the marketplace, and said to them, "You also go into the vineyard, and whatever is right I will give you." So they went. Again he went out about the sixth and the ninth hour, and did likewise. And about the eleventh hour he went out and found others standing idle, and said to them, "Why have you been standing here idle all day?" They said to him, "Because no one hired us." He said to them, "You also go into the vineyard, and whatever is right you will receive."

So when evening had come, the owner of the vineyard said to his steward, "Call the laborers and give them their wages, beginning with the last to the first." And when those came who were hired about the eleventh hour, they each received a denarius. But when the first came, they supposed that they would receive more; and they likewise received each a denarius. And when they had received it, they complained against the landowner, saying, "These last men have worked only one hour, and you made them equal to us who have borne the burden and the heat of the day." But he answered one of them and said, "Friend, I am doing you no wrong. Did you not agree with me for a denarius? Take what is yours and go your way. I wish to give to this last man the same as to you. Is it not lawful for me to do what I wish with my own things? Or is your eye evil because I am good?" So the last will be first, and the first last. For many are called, but few chosen.
(MATTHEW 20:1–16)

Does this parable upset us?

There are two ways of looking at this employer. One is that he is a very gracious man, and we should praise him for his kindness. The other is that he is an unfair man because he did not give more to those who worked longer. God's gift of worth has the same two responses. Some call it wondrously good, and some call it evil. Notice who in this parable thought their master was evil. It was those who worked more and thus thought they were worth more. Those who got a denarius for much less work were probably singing the praises of their boss.

Jesus's parable spoke to the people of that day and it still speaks in our day. The ones who thought they had earned more because

55

of who they were or what they did opposed Jesus the most. Grace offended them. Why should they trade their kingdom where worth is earned for one where it is a gift? This would elevate the sinners to the same level of favor they enjoyed. Unthinkable! Unfair!

We may protest, too. We might concede that the threat of punishment is not a very good motivator to live for God. Fear can make us do what is required, but it can never compel us to love God. We can do without the threat of wrath, but we cannot do without the promise of reward, can we? If we do not get a bigger mansion in heaven for serving God on Earth, why serve Him at all? We need some way to indicate we are better than the other guy.

Those who must have this kind of payment to serve God do not fully understand the kingdom. Love is its own reward. For example, those of us who have children spend countless hours pouring out our lives for their benefit. When it is done, we do not hold out our hand for a payback that would cheapen our love. Having the privilege of loving them is our satisfaction, and we need nothing else.

Those who love *have God* for God is love; loving is participating in God's gift. Those who love *partake of God*, and He is their reward and greatest possession. The finest mansion in heaven cannot compare to the glory of love. Consequently, if we dwell in God's kingdom, we hope that the fellow who has done less than us gets the same reward as we do. Love would have it no other way.

A Story to Ponder

I had a dream I walked with Jesus.
I asked Him to show me the beauty of His kingdom.
I expected to see a perfect world
Where there were no unlovable people,
Where everyone agreed on everything,
Where no one did wrong,
But most of all, I envisioned a place
Where I never failed my Lord again.
Then Jesus began to show me His kingdom:
I saw the homeless,
The imprisoned,
The enslaved,
And the outcasts.
I looked into the eyes of my worst enemy;
I saw my own weakness,
My worst fears,
And my greatest failures.
I begged the Lord to stop—
How could this be the kingdom?
It is so...ugly!
Then Jesus opened my eyes:
I saw how he loved the outcasts,
The sinners,
The enslaved.
He died for his enemies.
He died for me.
I fell to my knees and worshipped.
How beautiful is Your kingdom, Lord!
How beautiful is the kingdom of God!

Opposition to the Gift

We can learn much about a person by who loves him and who hates him. We might think those who opposed Jesus were the "the worst" sinners, such as tax collectors, murderers, thieves, and prostitutes. We might also think that those who loved Him were good people who tried their best to keep God's commandments. One of the greatest ironies of the Bible is that the opposite was often true. Those who thought they were on God's side usually fought the hardest against the kingdom of God, while those thought to be on the Devil's side rejoiced at its coming.

We would do well to ponder this great paradox, for if we understand what it meant to fight God in Jesus's day, we can learn what it means to fight God in our day. We do not want to be like those who believed they were working for God but were actually working against Him.

The Pharisees

Jesus called those who were alive at His coming a "wicked generation,"[1] and we might conclude that these people were doing a whole lot of sinning. While that generation certainly did its share of Law breaking, it may have been the most zealous for God's Law in Israel's history. Men like the Pharisees were determined to be the best Torah keepers possible. To them, righteousness was found in the details.[2]

God gave the Law through Moses about 1500 years earlier, but God's commandments were a little vague on some things. For example, the Torah strictly forbade working on God's holy day. God was so adamant about keeping the Sabbath that breaking it carried the death penalty. Yet how were God's people to decide what qualified as work and what did not?

Over a period of generations, men like the Pharisees added definition to the Law. By the time of Christ, they had thirty-nine categories of things a person could not do on the Sabbath, including how far a person could walk. According to Jewish traditions, if a person took one step over 2000 cubits, he violated God's day of rest. How did they come up with this number? When the Hebrew people were wandering in the wilderness, God told them to carry the Ark of the Covenant exactly 2000 cubits in front of the people. Obviously, He was also telling them how far they could walk on the Sabbath. (Well, maybe that is not so obvious!)

The Pharisees' requirements covered big and small things alike. For instance, God's holy day was not a good day to get sick or suffer an accident, as they forbade healing on the Sabbath. Their rules also addressed mundane tasks, such as knot tying. A true Torah keeper could not tie or untie a knot on the sacred day.

Of course, there were differing interpretations of the Law, and some were stricter than others. A group of folks called the Essenes were so strict that they would not even allow wool to remain in dye over the Sabbath because the dye itself was working. As you can see, it took a whole lot of work *not* to work.

We might think such efforts to keep Torah down to the smallest detail impressed Jesus— but we would be wrong. In fact, the Lord deliberately broke the oral traditions of the Pharisees every chance He got. Jesus's miracles were not random works of power but *living illustrations* of God's grace, saying something directly to the self-righteous of the day. And His message was not so kind.

Now as Jesus passed by, He saw a man who was blind from birth. And His disciples asked Him, saying, "Rabbi, who sinned, this man or his parents, that he was born blind?"

Jesus answered, "Neither this man nor his parents sinned, but that the works of God should be revealed in him. I must work the works of Him who sent Me while it is day; the night is coming when no one can work. As long as I am in the world, I am the light of the world."

When He had said these things, He spat on the ground and made clay with the saliva; and He anointed the eyes of the blind man with the clay. And He said to him, "Go, wash in the Pool of Siloam" (which is translated, Sent). So he went and washed, and came back seeing.

Therefore the neighbors and those who previously had seen that he was blind said, "Is not this he who sat and begged?"

Some said, "This is he." Others said, "He is like him."

He said, "I am he."

Therefore they said to him, "How were your eyes opened?"

He answered and said, "A Man called Jesus made clay and anointed my eyes and said to me, 'Go to the Pool of Siloam and wash.' So I went and washed, and I received sight."

Then they said to him, "Where is He?"

He said, "I do not know."

They brought him who formerly was blind to the Pharisees. Now it was a Sabbath when Jesus made the clay and opened his eyes. Then the Pharisees also asked him again how he had received his sight. He said to them, "He put clay on my eyes, and I washed, and I see."

Therefore some of the Pharisees said, "This Man is not from God, because He does not keep the Sabbath." (JOHN 9:1–16)

When we understand the traditions of the day, we see that Jesus's act of kindness was also a deliberate insult to the Pharisees. This was one of Jesus's many provocative miracles. The Pharisees declared that it was unlawful to heal on the Sabbath, but if we study the Gospels, we see that Jesus's *favorite day* to heal was the Sabbath. This was no accident. Notice His marvelous play on words at the beginning of this passage: "I must work the works of Him who sent Me while it is day; the night is coming when no one can work." In other words, it was the day of rest, but Jesus was about to get busy.

The way Jesus healed this man may seem strange until we understand that the Lord's method was meant to provoke. He spat on the ground, made a paste, and rubbed it in the man's eyes. Some say there was something magical about the saliva or the mud—maybe it had some healing powers that we do not comprehend. However, the reason Jesus put mud in the man's eyes is probably much less mystical. He wanted to tick off the Pharisees. According to the legal climate, making paste as Jesus did was working on the Sabbath.

Finally, the Lord told the man to go wash in the Pool of Siloam to activate the man's faith, right? That sounds spiritual, but it is more likely Jesus was just up to more mischief. Reading John, chapter 8, we see this miracle probably took place in the vicinity of the Temple. And guess how far it was to the Pool of Siloam and back? It just happened to be more than the allotted 2000 cubits!

Jesus deliberately broke the Pharisees' traditions not once but *three times* with just one miracle. And this was not the only time Jesus provoked the religious leaders of the day; it seems it was one of His favorite pastimes.

In John, chapter 5, we read the story of Jesus's encounter with a lame man at the Pool of Bethesda. The Lord told the man to take up his bed and walk, and immediately, the fellow was healed. The Lord could have said, "Get up and walk," but He also told the man to take up his bed. Again, this was deliberate, as taking up one's bed on the day of rest was "working."

Jesus angered the Pharisees with His miracles as well as the company He kept. Known as "a glutton and a winebibber [one who drinks a lot of wine],"[3] He earned this reputation by regularly dining with the worst sinners. Apparently, these meals were not solemn occasions but lively celebrations of the kingdom of God. Unlike the Jews, who would not allow "unworthy" people such as the tax collectors to worship in the Temple with the Torah keepers, Jesus treated these outcasts like brothers, seeking them out. And when He found them, He gave them an embrace, not a rebuke. Eating a meal with someone in that day meant friendship, acceptance, and even love, and the Pharisees could not stomach Jesus's kindness.

How could Jesus welcome sinners but provoke the righteous? To some, it appeared He was spitting on the Torah. No wonder many people said He was of the Devil.[4] He certainly appeared to be on the sinners' side.

Was Jesus saying it was better to be a Torah breaker than a Torah keeper? To answer this question, we must understand Jesus's mission. Jesus was not endorsing sin and neither was He against zeal for God's Law; He came to make God's approval a gift. Quite simply, those who opposed Him opposed the gift and those who loved Him loved the gift; herein was the dividing line. Grace was coming, and if people embraced it, they saw the kingdom of God; if they stood in its way, they could get flattened. When we grasp this, we understand Jesus's relationships. Very good people often have a hard time with grace, and thus the Pharisees had a hard time with Jesus.

Also He spoke this parable to some who trusted in themselves that they were righteous and despised others: Two men went up to the temple to pray, one a Pharisee and the other a tax collector. The Pharisee stood and prayed thus with himself, "God, I thank You that I am not like other men—extortioners, unjust, adulterers, or even as this tax collector. I fast twice a week; I give tithes of all that I possess." And the tax collector, standing afar off, would not so much as raise his eyes to heaven, but beat his breast, saying, "God, be merciful to me a sinner!" I tell you, this man went down to his house justified rather than the other; for everyone who exalts himself will be humbled, and he who humbles himself will be exalted. (LUKE 18:9–14)

The Pharisees stressed two things in their religious devotion: fasting and tithing. The average Pharisee fasted two days a week and paid his tithes faithfully. The fellow in Jesus's story sounds like the perfect church member, yet God didn't want him around. Even with all this fellow's good deeds, he opposed Christ. On the other hand, the tax collector was one of the most flawed men in the land, yet he found the kingdom of God.

Ironically, religion is often God's worst enemy. In the Gospels, we never see Jesus rebuke the worst sinners of the day. We see no long speeches against the tax collectors or the prostitutes, and He had no unkind words for the pagan Romans. Many wanted Him to speak against Caesar, but His only commentary on the matter was "Render, therefore, to Caesar the things that are Caesar's, and to God the things that are God's."[5] On the other hand, Jesus had scathing rebukes and threats for the religious leaders of His time. He said they were "whitewashed tombs," the blind leading the blind, and the sons of the Devil. Just before the cross, Jesus said the punishment would come upon them for all the righteous blood shed upon the Earth.[6]

Religion often opposes God because of its tendency to focus on self-righteousness. Self-righteousness—self taking the place of Christ—is man's attempt to gain what God has already given, and that is the antithesis of the gift. If we trust in ourselves that we are righteous, we cannot trust Christ to be our righteousness. Surprisingly, those who seek God's approval through their good deeds are running *away* from God, not toward Him. To know union with Christ, we must partake of Christ's own standing with the Father. To make self the measure of our acceptance is to exalt self above God; it is rejecting Christ rather than accepting Him. Quite possibly this is humanity's greatest war with God. Who is our righteousness? Is it self or is it Christ?

Self-righteousness is always accompanied by contempt. God was *accepting*; the Pharisees were rejecting, and as such, the Pharisees opposed the very nature of the kingdom of God. Satan's favorite attire is religion, for it can be destructive to relationship with both God and man. The worst sins cannot keep a person out of the kingdom of God but self-righteousness can.

The parable of the prodigal son[7] beautifully illustrates the nature of the Pharisees. When we hear sermons about this story, we mostly hear about the younger, more sinful brother. Everyone seems to be able to relate to this fellow, but the parable is about *two* brothers and their relationships with their father. We do not hear much about the older brother, who stayed at home and did everything right. I think we overlook or ignore him because we do not quite know what to do with this young man. He was a good guy, but at the end of the story, we see him isolated from both his father and his brother.

When the prodigal returned, the father, overwhelmed with love, threw a grand party for his wayward son; the older brother was the party pooper. The eldest son could not stand his father lavishly loving someone who did not deserve it, and he was angry with his fallen brother, too. At the end of the story, the father reached out to his older son, but the parable concludes with his son's fate uncertain.

The Pharisees thought they were the life of God's party, but they were among the biggest party poopers of all. This is the great deception of self-righteousness: it is hatred for God masquerading as love.

The Sadducees and the Priesthood

The Sadducees and the priesthood ran the Temple and were almost synonymous. There was no separation between church and state in that day. The priests at the Temple in Jerusalem not only officiated over the religious life of the Jews, they were also rulers and judges.

King Herod, who was himself a pawn of Rome, installed his own pawns in the Jewish priesthood. By the first century, choosing the High Priest was as much political as it was religious. Herod needed to support Rome to survive, so he made sure the priesthood also supported Rome. It would be unfair to categorize all of the priesthood as sympathetic to Caesar, however. Some were in favor of rebellion, but those at the highest levels were undoubtedly in Rome's back pocket. We see evidence of this loyalty to and fear of Rome in the Gospels.

Then many of the Jews who had come to Mary, and had seen the things Jesus did, believed in Him. But some of them went away to the Pharisees and told them the things Jesus did.

Then the chief priests and the Pharisees gathered a council and said, "What shall we do? For this Man works many signs. If we let Him alone like this, everyone will believe in Him, and the Romans will come and take away both our place and nation." (JOHN 11:45–48)

But they cried out, "Away with Him, away with Him! Crucify Him!"

Pilate said to them, "Shall I crucify your King?" The chief priests answered, "We have no king but Caesar!"

Then he delivered Him to them to be crucified. Then they took Jesus and led Him away. (JOHN 19:15–16)

Josephus, the first-century historian, recorded that the priesthood went so far as to authorize a daily sacrifice for Caesar in the Temple. This was a source of continual angst for the Jews, and in the final Jewish–Roman conflict, the Jews stopped the daily ritual. Unfortunately, Rome considered this an act of war and eventually destroyed Jerusalem in retaliation.[8]

The priesthood also lived in luxury well beyond that of the average man. They supported their lavish lifestyles with a Temple tax, which every Jew was required to pay. Richard Horsley, in his book *The Message and the Kingdom*, describes what archeologists have discovered about the living conditions of the priesthood. The priests in Jerusalem lived in extravagant mansions with mosaic floors and magnificently carved wall decorations. They dined with elegant tableware and surrounded themselves with fine furnishings.

Jesus's popularity was undoubtedly a source of jealousy for the priesthood and the Sadducees, but their main motivation for seeking to kill Jesus was fear. When a new king came to power, he would set his version of the priesthood in place. All this talk of Jesus becoming the King of the Jews undoubtedly unnerved the priests in Jerusalem. If Jesus came to power, they thought they would be out of a job or killed. Plus, they knew the Romans did not take too kindly to unauthorized kings, so Jesus could invite the wrath of Rome as well.

The Pharisees opposed Jesus because they would not give up their own righteousness for the righteousness of Christ, and the Sadducees opposed Jesus because they thought He would cost them their possessions and their power. Indeed, following Christ meant putting God above their things. They could no longer define abundant life through their wealth and status; Christ would become their treasure and their life. Both these groups had a lot to lose in order to enter the kingdom of God, and both thought the price too high to pay.

The Pharisees and the Sadducees give us a picture of what it means to oppose the kingdom of God. Resistance to Christ is not always a matter of good deeds and bad deeds; sometimes it is better understood in terms of union and disunion. If self is our righteousness, we stand alone, without Christ. Likewise, if we look to material things for completion, we cannot know completion in Christ. God is very serious about giving Himself to us, and resistance to His gift is the essence of resistance to God.

The Herods and Caesar: Men Who Would Be Gods

Roman persecution against Christ's followers did not begin until after the Lord's death and resurrection, and it did not reach its full intensity until the latter half of the first century. In the Roman Empire, we see the pagan version of the exaltation of self over God.

The Herods were Rome's puppet rulers in Palestine. Herod the Great is the Herod we know best.[9] We remember him for killing all the boys in Bethlehem who were less than two years of age in an attempt to kill the Christ. The Jews believed their Messiah would not only be a Savior, but He would be King of the Jews. Herod no doubt looked at anyone claiming to be the Messiah as a rival.

Herod the Great was a brutal, paranoid ruler, and Josephus gives us a picture of this king's self-exaltation. Herod was afraid that there would be no mourning upon his death, so he gave orders that renowned and beloved men across the land would be put to death at his passing. In Herod's mind, this would ensure that the people would mourn at the death of the "great" king. Thankfully, no one carried out his orders.[10]

At Herod's death, Rome divided the kingdom among Herod's three sons—Antipas, Archelaus, and Philip—and none of them was any better than their father. Philip got the northeast region, and when he came to power, he changed the name of the city Paneas to Caesarea Philippi: "Caesarea" to honor Caesar and "Philippi," to honor himself. It was in this city that Peter received the revelation that Jesus was the Messiah, and here that the Lord proclaimed that gates of Hades would not prevail against His church.

After Herod the Great's death, the Jews did not have an official king over the land until AD 41, when the Romans gave Agrippa, Herod the Great's grandson, the throne. Agrippa truly thought himself to be divine. Josephus records that he wore a tightly woven, pure silver suit in public to make himself look heavenly. When he spoke, he stood so the sun would reflect on the silver and give him a shiny appearance.[11] In Acts, chapter 12, we see many did refer to Agrippa as a god, but the Lord only allowed the pompous king's arrogance to continue for a short time.

The scriptures give many names to Christ—King of Kings, Lord of Lords, Prince of Peace—but in the first century, someone else carried these exact titles. It was the Roman ruler Caesar. Rome declared that Caesar was a god who ruled over all the kings of the Earth, and He alone would bring peace to humanity.[12] In keeping with this philosophy, temples were scattered throughout the known world where people could worship the divine Caesar.

Early Christians were model citizens. They paid their taxes because their Lord told them to, and they were entirely nonviolent. While others in Palestine plotted against Rome, not one Christian raised a sword against Caesar. Yet the church did take issue with Rome. The Romans said Caesar was lord over all, and God's people proclaimed Christ as King of Kings. A conflict ensued that would reach its peak with the cruelest persecutor of all, Nero.

Historians wonder if some Roman emperors were insane, but there can be no doubt with Nero. Nero believed he was the son of the Greek god Apollo and fancied himself a divinely inspired musician and artist. To demonstrate these heavenly "gifts," Nero held one-man performances that lasted for hours—and they were unbearably awful. But his audiences were held captive, not by Nero's talent but by fear, as the penalty for walking out on the emperor was death. Some attendees devised a way to leave without punishment by faking their death, falling as if slain by the majesty of Nero's music and poetry. Others stayed and endured no matter what. There are even accounts of women giving birth during Nero's shows. When the emperor said you could not leave, he meant it.

Nero believed the city of Rome needed to be rebuilt to reflect his divine inspiration, and historians think he had the city set aflame to make room for his masterpiece. It is from this that we get the famous image of Nero fiddling while Rome burned. For the scheme to succeed, however, the emperor needed someone to blame. So, he picked a people who had no hope of defending themselves: the Christians.

It was Nero who first threw Christians to the lions for sport. In the great Circus Maximus, he had countless Christians killed by wild beasts, crucified, burned to death, and executed by the sword. Nero himself often dressed as a wild animal with steel claws and participated in the carnage. Then at night, he had believers boiled in oil and used as human torches to light his gardens. Although Nero's persecution was brief, lasting only four years, it is still the most horrific persecution against Christianity in history.

The scriptures say God humbles the proud, and this was certainly Nero's fate. Rome turned against him, and while his enemies pursued him, he killed himself with his own sword. Today, a great stone pillar from the center of Nero's Circus Maximus stands in the courtyard of St. Peter's Basilica in Rome. An inscription has been chiseled into the stone that says (translated): "Christ is conquering. Christ is reigning. Christ rules over all."[13]

We could view the battle between Caesar and Christ as a fight for status—as if God needed to prove that He was bigger than any person. God has no such ego problems. The problem with self-exaltation is that it is the nemesis of grace, and those who place themselves above God cannot have God. Surprisingly, those who put themselves below God cannot have Him either. Our place is *at God's side*, and Christ's love is what puts us there.[14]

No doubt, others like the Pharisees and Sadducees thought themselves better than the arrogant Herods and the pagan Caesars, but really, all these people had the same sin in different forms: they could not take their eyes off themselves to look at Christ. Therefore, they could not see that the true Savior and King had come. When we exalt ourselves above God or above our brother, we are at war with love, and that is a war no one can win.

Ever since the day of Adam, humanity has opposed God, but that opposition usually takes forms we do not recognize. We look for the battle of good versus evil, but this is not the heart of our fight with God. Men like the Pharisees, the Sadducees, the Herods, and the Caesars are no longer around, but our opposition to the gift takes the same forms. When we fight God's gift, we also fight each other; we fight over whom God loves best. Those who have the world's definition of the good life protect it at all costs, and those who do not have it will often obtain it at another's expense. We define power as being above others, but this means another must be considered weak.

Jesus brought a new definition of what it means to oppose God. He also brought a new definition of what it means to be "right." It is to His definition that we now turn.

— 6 —

The Kingdom of God Is Bigger Than Being Right

Two great leaders of the Reformation were Martin Luther and Ulrich Zwingli. In their day, reformers were still taking their first steps away from the church at Rome, but Protestants also wasted no time in dividing among each other. And at the center of Protestant doctrinal disputes were Luther and Zwingli. Luther headed the German Reformation, and Zwingli the Swiss.

In an effort to unite Protestantism, a man named Philipp of Hesse invited the contrary theologians to meet at a conference in Marburg, Germany. After days of work, the two reached an agreement on every issue but one, the nature of communion. When the conference was over, because of this one matter, one man refused to shake the other's hand. If there was ever a chance of the Protestant Church being one, it was lost that day.[1]

Each of these great reformers thought he knew God better than the other. Yet did these men act like they knew the Lord? If they did, certainly they would have left the conference as brothers rather than enemies. We can only wonder what Protestantism would be like today if the two had accepted each other in spite of their differences. Instead, Protestants continued to divide into what has become thousands of denominations.

The gift of God's acceptance opens the door to accepting one another, too. Our differing beliefs so readily close what God has opened, however. The quest for light and truth is a good endeavor, but if we are not careful, it can lead us into the darkest parts of human nature. To understand why something as good as doctrine can have such bad consequences, it helps to understand how our minds work in the twenty-first century.

We are all subject to a paradigm, and our paradigm is *the way we think*. It influences everything from our culture to how we interpret the meaning of words. The book of Proverbs tells us that as a man "thinks in his heart, so is he."[2] Whether we will admit it or not, we all have a mindset, and it helps to shape who we are.

The roots of today's Western mind extend back to ancient Greece—we are Hellenized in our thinking. Though folks like Aristotle, Socrates, and Plato lived a very long time ago, their influence on our worldview remains.[3] Out of ancient Greek thought came the medieval paradigm and then the modern paradigm. We live in a society that is a mix of modern and postmodern thought, and Western society has changed its mind many times. Whenever this happened, those of the old or previous paradigm thought those of the new had lost their minds. The time of Luther and Zwingli, the modern mind was flexing its muscles, exercising two characteristics of the modern paradigm: rationalism and individualism.

If someone in the ancient world experienced a thunderstorm, he might think some deity was displeased or speaking in some way. In the Old Testament, the false god Baal was the god of thunder, and the Canaanites believed a lightning storm was their god sounding off. Today, we think such thoughts are foolish—everyone knows thunderstorms happen when cold and warm air collide, right? When the ancient and medieval paradigms gave way to the modern mind, the supernatural gave way to the natural.

Additionally, we in the modern world are much more individualistic than our ancient brothers. We tend to define ourselves by what makes us unique, believing our individual talents, personalities, and opinions make us who we are. Thoughts like "I am who I am" come straight from the modern paradigm; we believe our opinion is the most important opinion. We also think our views are between God and us, so no one has the right to tell us what to believe. With the rise of individualism, concepts such as the priesthood of every believer came into focus. We proclaim that everyone has his or her own relationship with God, and we do not need someone to have a relationship with the Lord for us. We can all come boldly before God's throne of grace.

The ancient world was much more corporate in its mindset. People who lived then would not look at themselves to find their identity as much as they would to their corporate community. We see this in the Apostle Paul's "body talk."[4] He said that Christians are part of the body of Christ, and being part of the whole defined who they were as individuals. For example, the body of Christ is favored and blessed, so each of its members is favored and blessed. The ancient world found its definition not as much in the "I" as in the "we."

With the rise of the modern paradigm, the natural began to infringe upon the supernatural, and the "I" upon the "we." This opened up many possibilities for good, but it also created new problems. And there was no place where these difficulties were more evident than in the church. Suddenly, in the eyes of many, a new threat to faith appeared: science! As natural explanations replaced supernatural explanations, it appeared humanity was kicking God out of the cosmos. The more we learned how things work, it seemed the less we needed God.

This feud between rational and mystical thought has continued for generations, and it is only recently that many are seeing that the natural and the supernatural need not be enemies. In fact, they can be *partners* in revealing God's glory. As we discover more about the universe, we are seeing that God is more awesome than we ever imagined; the way the world exists and operates is a far greater miracle than the thunder god shouting in a storm.[5]

With the rise in rational thinking came an increased focus on hermeneutics (the science of interpretation) and critical analysis as people set out to better understand the Bible. Many believed that as we studied the scriptures, correct interpretations would become obvious and a united church would follow. We would all be on the same page with the same doctrine, and a glorious new day would begin.

However, there were other forces at work. The invention of the printing press put the Bible in the hands of the common person, revolutionizing Christianity and launching a golden age of evangelism. With each copy of a Bible came an individual opinion about its interpretation, however, and the doctrine that was supposed to bring people together ended up having the opposite effect. Protestants began to divide, and denominations were born in the aftermath of church split after church split.

Some still say a common interpretation of the scriptures is what will bring us together. One system of understanding just needs to dominate the others with the force of reason, and eventually the best argument will win. Others have acknowledged that individualism is too powerful, believing the only way we can have unity is to throw out the divisive idea of absolute truth. Everyone has his or her own version of the truth, and we should just leave it at that.

Consider looking at this problem another way: what we need to throw out is not truth but self-righteousness. Self-righteousness is the self masquerading as God. In Jesus's day, when people like the Pharisees condemned others for not keeping Torah, they thought they were holding up God's standard. In reality, they were making *themselves* the standard. If they were really holding up God's Law, it would have revealed that they needed grace just as much as anyone else.

Self-righteousness does not always have to be about behavior; it can also be about beliefs. Just as the Pharisees thought their superior deeds brought them closer to God, some today think their superior doctrines make them God's favorites. These Pharisees of the modern paradigm make their own understanding the yardstick by which they measure others: there are those who are right and there are those who are wrong, and God loves one and hates the other. This is the same "us and them" of the first century in different clothing. It is still self-righteousness and it is still contrary to grace. If our closeness to God is God's accomplishment, there is no room for boasting, either in our deeds or in our understanding.

Accepting God's gift does not mean our beliefs and actions do not matter, however. The search for understanding is one of the noblest pursuits in life, but we must be careful where this journey takes us. If our quest for truth is our attempt to grasp God, it will most certainly lead us away from God no matter how pure our doctrine becomes.

Any efforts to corral or obtain God, whether through good behavior or good understanding, invariably lead to self-righteousness. We will always look down upon those who do not comprehend God as well as we do. Alternately, when we see God has grasped us in Christ, the shackles of self-righteousness fall away, and we are free to love God and our neighbor. His hold on us matters far more than our hold on Him. 1 Corinthians 13, the love chapter, speaks of these things:

> And though I have the gift of prophecy, and understand all mysteries and all knowledge, and though I have all faith, so that I could remove mountains, but have not love, I am nothing. (1 CORINTHIANS 13:2)

If our advanced understanding leads us to hate, what good is it? Great wisdom should not cause us to devalue our brother; it should open our eyes to our brother's worth. If we think understanding the Bible makes us better than our brother, we do not understand the Bible at all.

Someone once called me a "book snob." I think it was because this person always saw me carrying around books that were as heavy in physical weight as they were in theological content. Ordinary books that everyone else was reading would not do. I had to be on the cutting edge of the best ideas about God.

Knowing a lot about the scriptures impresses people, and when I was very young, people told me I had wisdom far beyond my years. Knowing more gave me a place in people's hearts, and I thought it would give me a place in God's heart, too. In my mind, being close to God was just one more revelation or one more book away.

Unfortunately, I did not understand one of the most important concepts: what impresses people does not impress God. The Lord wanted me to see something, but its wisdom was so simple a child could grasp it. In fact, many of "the least of these" understood God's mind far better than me. I did not need another book, another good deed, or another spiritual experience to get close to the Lord; the

Lord's presence is a gift God gave a long time ago at a place called Calvary. I spent years trying to learn or work my way closer to God. What I needed was to see that I was already there.

I still enjoy being on the cutting edge of the latest "educated" thoughts on God, but now my view is very different. Instead of seeing myself as special because of my knowledge, I see how special everyone is because of Christ, and it is a sight to behold. This is perhaps what Jesus saw when He looked at the Torah breakers of His day, and this is what we should see when we look at those with less-than-perfect doctrine today.

A little help from our ancient friends can help us determine what it truly means to *know God.* Their words reveal that knowing God is far more than having good doctrine.

> *Beloved, let us love one another, for love is of God; and everyone who loves is born of God and knows God. He who does not love does not know God, for God is love.* (1 JOHN 4:7–8)

John's statement illustrates another difference between the ancient Hebrew mind and the modern mind. We often equate "knowing" with having our facts straight and believe we can come to know something by reading a book or by listening to a teacher's lecture. To the ancients this alone was not knowing; to them, knowing was *participating in and partaking of something.* For example, when the Bible says a man "knew his wife," it was not saying he had read a book about her!

We see this in the first-century rabbi/disciple relationship. A disciple's goal was, of course, to learn a bunch of facts from his rabbi, but he did so in tandem with the goal of becoming like his instructor in every way possible.[6] A successful disciple was one who could both pass an exam *and* behave like his teacher.

Understanding the ancient concept of what it means "to know" brings to life John's statement about knowing God. Biblically, a person who knows God is not the one with perfect doctrine; knowing God is *participation in who God is.* Therefore, if God is love, the measure of how much we know Him is how much we love.

We sometimes wonder why God loves us, looking at ourselves to try to find the answer. Commonly, we take stock of our good deeds and our good doctrines, but the better place to look is at God. He loves us because, wonder of wonders, He is love. We can no more stop God from loving us than we can stop God from being Himself. He is what He is, and He has given us no say in the matter. Therefore, His love is without "becauses." God does not say, "I love you because you do this or because you think that." He simply says, "I love you."

Most of the people reading this book do not know me, the author, very well. On these pages are my best thoughts and ideas, and if someone only sees my best, they might find me easy to love. My friends, on the other hand, know my best as well as a little of my worst. Still, they love me. And it is a small miracle that my wife, who knows more of my worst than anybody, loves me. (She might say that it is a big miracle!)

God is in a category all by Himself because He fully knows us and fully loves us *no matter what*. It has been said that if our friends could read our minds, we would not have any friends. *Nothing* is hidden from the Lord; He knows my thoughts and all I have ever done or ever will do. Yet He loves me more than anyone does. Astonishing!

Because God loves us so, the more we know Him, the more we love without "becauses." And if God is our reason not to love people, the image we have of God is not God.

You have heard that it was said, "You shall love your neighbor and hate your enemy." But I say to you, love your enemies, bless those who curse you, do good to those who hate you, and pray for those who spitefully use you and persecute you, that you may be sons of your Father in heaven; for He makes His sun rise on the evil and on the good, and sends rain on the just and on the unjust. For if you love those who love you, what reward have you? Do not even the tax collectors do the same? And if you greet your brethren only, what do you do more than others? Do not even the tax collectors do so? Therefore you shall be perfect, just as your Father in heaven is perfect. (MATTHEW 5:43–48)

Jesus said we are to love our enemies, though He could just as easily have said that we are to love those who disagree with us. Which is the greater proof that we know God, loving someone with whom we agree or loving someone with whom we disagree?

The kingdom of God is not the dominance of one idea or doctrine over another; it is the reign of love. We see this clearly in the parable of the Good Samaritan.

And behold, a certain lawyer stood up and tested Him, saying, "Teacher, what shall I do to inherit eternal life?"

He said to him, "What is written in the law? What is your reading of it?"

So he answered and said, "'You shall love the Lord your God with all your heart, with all your soul, with all your strength, and with all your mind,' and 'your neighbor as yourself.'"

And He said to him, "You have answered rightly; do this and you will live."

But he, wanting to justify himself, said to Jesus, "And who is my neighbor?"

Then Jesus answered and said: "A certain man went down from Jerusalem to Jericho, and fell among thieves, who stripped him of his clothing, wounded him, and departed, leaving him half dead. Now by chance a certain priest came down that road. And when he saw him, he passed by on the other side. Likewise a Levite, when he arrived at the place, came and looked, and passed by on the other side. But a certain Samaritan, as he journeyed, came where he was. And when he saw him, he had compassion. So he went to him and bandaged his wounds, pouring on oil and wine; and he set him on his own animal, brought him to an inn, and took care of him. On the next day, when he departed, he took out two denarii, gave them to the innkeeper, and said to him, 'Take care of him; and whatever more you spend, when I come again, I will repay you.' So which of these three do you think was neighbor to him who fell among the thieves?"

And he said, "He who showed mercy on him."

Then Jesus said to him, "Go and do likewise." (LUKE 10:25–37)

We often read of the regions of Judea, Samaria, and Galilee in the Gospels because each had its own predominant religious climate. The Judeans, for instance, thought they had a lot going for them because they kept their Hebrew heritage intact more than people in the other regions of Palestine and they could confidently boast that they were pureblooded descendants of Abraham. Judea was also the home to Jerusalem, God's most holy city, and the Temple, which was the center of Jewish religious life. To many, being closer to the Temple meant being closer to God. It is no wonder some Judeans thought they were God's favorites.

To the far north was Galilee. The Galileans were not quite as pure as their Judean neighbors to the south, as they tended to be more Hellenized or Greek in their thinking. The folks in Judea might have accepted the Galileans, but just barely.

Sandwiched between the two other regions, the Samaritans were in a different class altogether. They had intermarried heavily with pagans, and they had some pretty strange ideas. They practiced some of the Jewish customs, but their neighbors to the north and south believed their estranged brothers did things all wrong. The Samaritans built their own temple on Mount Gerizim, for example. The Temple was supposed to be in Jerusalem, but the Jewish inhabitants of Samaria believed Mount Gerizim was God's chosen place and the only true center for worship. They called it the "navel of the Earth" because they believed that Adam sacrificed there. To the Samaritans, Moses was the only prophet and intercessor in the final judgment, so they limited the scriptures to the Pentateuch. And they followed their strange beliefs and strange practices with a strange eschatology (beliefs about the end of the world, judgment, and the resurrection). The Samaritans were certain that 6,000 years after creation, a Restorer would come and live on Earth for 110 years. On the judgment day, God would resurrect the righteous to paradise and cast the wicked into eternal fire.[7]

The Samaritans had bad doctrine, and the Judeans hated them. If a Judean needed to travel north to Galilee, he would take a much longer and more dangerous route *around* Samaria. In contrast, the Gospels often portray the Samaritans as heroes, and this alone should tell us something about the nature of the kingdom of God.

Jesus filled His parables with irony, and none is more ironic than the story of the Good Samaritan. Since the priests were intercessors between the Lord and His people, they were closest to God—or so people thought. The next closest might be the Levites, who assisted the priesthood, and without a doubt, the furthest from God were the Samaritans, who could not get anything right. Yet who was right in this parable? Who really knew God?

Jesus told this story to answer the lawyer's question, "Who is my neighbor;" in other words, "Who should I love as myself?" Jesus came to make the neighborhood bigger than anyone imagined, and it included the Samaritans and, later, the most unloved of all, the Gentiles. And still today, the kingdom of God extends far beyond being right, offering the greatest proof of its presence through loving people who are wrong.

We tend to believe that Christians have to be alike to be one, so we create "statements of faith" to make sure we are all on the same page. In Jesus's day, this would be like making the Samaritans the same as the Judeans so Israel could be one. "We" would triumph over "I," and there would be peace—supposedly.

Such methods always fail, however. In fact, the more we seek docturnal unity, the more it seems to elude us. We have the choice to fight for "the truth," isolating ourselves in ever smaller circles of fellowship, or we can take up the greater challenge of God's kingdom: we can make it our goal *not* to get everyone on the same page but to *love those with whom we disagree.* In doing so, God will open our eyes to *truth that goes beyond being right.* Just as love covers a multitude of sins, it also covers bad doctrine, freeing us to see those who are "wrong" as our brethren.

Jesus did not come to make the Samaritans like the Judeans or the Jews like the Gentiles; *He came to bring a kingdom where diverse people can love each other as if they were alike.* He did this by making our unity His accomplishment on the cross 2000 years ago. Who Jesus is and what He has done makes us one. Our unity, like God's love, simply *is.*

— 7 —

The Cross

I was scarcely ten years old when I came to Christ. The church I attended required all new believers to attend a pastor's class. I don't remember the pastor's name, but I do remember something he said even though it was some forty years ago. He said that Christ identified with us, so we could identify with Christ. I did not understand what he was talking about, but for some reason, those words stuck with me. In this chapter, we are going to talk about their meaning.

No one viewpoint or image can fully convey the meaning of the cross of Christ. Moreover, one lifetime is not enough to grasp its fullness. The significance of Calvary is something we should ponder and wrestle with our whole lives. All that we are and all that we have is tied to what happened when Jesus died and rose from the grave.

The cross is the triumph of God. And the greatest irony in history may be the Lord's use of the cross—a highly shameful instrument associated with failure and defeat—to bring about absolute victory for Himself and for all humanity.

The most common understanding of the atonement is what the scholars call "penal substitution."[1] In other words, Christ came to take the punishment for sin in our place to save us from the wrath of God. In the New Testament, we see Christ, our Passover Lamb, dying for our sins,[2] and this image takes us back to the time of the

Exodus: God's tenth and most horrible plague was about to come upon the Egypt, and the Angel of Death was coming to take the firstborn son from every family. To escape the Lord's wrath, Moses told the people to take the blood from a spotless lamb and place it on the door to their home. When the Angel of Death saw the blood, he would pass over the marked house and spare the child. This is a marvelous picture of Jesus, God's firstborn, who shed His blood to save us.

Modern illustrations of the cross include that of a courtroom drama. A man is condemned to death for crimes he has committed, and it seems he has no way of escape, no hope of reprieve. At the last minute, out of love, another man stands up and says, "I will take the blame for this man's wrongs. I will pay the price. Punish me instead!"

Such images help us understand that Christ suffered in our place, bearing the consequences of our sin. At the cross, God treated His sinless son like a sinner, pouring out His wrath on His firstborn. When we should have been the ones left isolated from God and humanity, God delivered the agony of Calvary upon His Son instead. The prophet Isaiah foretold the Lord's suffering:

Surely He has borne our griefs

And carried our sorrows;

Yet we esteemed Him stricken,

Smitten by God, and afflicted.

But He was wounded for our transgressions,

He was bruised for our iniquities;

The chastisement for our peace was upon Him,

And by His stripes we are healed.

All we like sheep have gone astray;

We have turned, every one, to his own way;

And the Lord has laid on Him the iniquity of us all.
(ISAIAH 53:4–6)

The book of Hebrews provides another perspective on how Christ took our place. Speaking of Jesus, it says, "...but now, once at the end of the ages, He has appeared to put away sin by the sacrifice of Himself."[3] At first glance, this passage may seem a bit confusing— "put away sin"? Does this mean that Christ came so we would not sin anymore? If that is so, we might think Jesus was a failure since we all still sin.

A better way of looking at this concept is that Jesus put away *the power* of sin. We still sin, but *sin has lost its power over us.* Before Christ came, sin was like a cruel master who held us captive; it enslaved us and kept us from going where we wanted. God illustrated the nature of sin's tyranny in the Old Testament Temple. The central court in God's house was the Holiest of Holies, and beyond its veil was the presence of God. Yet no one could go in there, save the High Priest of Israel, and he only did so once a year, to offer a sacrifice for the people. The veil surrounding God's glory was a living picture of the power of sin: sin said "You can't go in there," and humanity had no choice but to obey. This is the tyranny of sin.

At the cross, Jesus took our sins upon Himself and allowed Himself to fall into sin's grasp. He felt, for the first time, the sting of separation from His Father, and He cried out, "My God, my God, why have you forsaken me?"[4]

The Lord bore our isolation from God at Calvary so that, when Christ died, our separation from God would die with Him—sin would lose its grip on humanity. From that day forward, though sin still exists, it is powerless to keep us from God's presence.

Seeing then that we have a great High Priest who has passed through the heavens, Jesus the Son of God, let us hold fast our confession. For we do not have a High Priest who cannot sympathize with our weaknesses, but was in all points tempted as we are, yet without sin. Let us therefore come boldly to the throne of grace, that we may obtain mercy and find grace to help in time of need. (HEBREWS 4:14–16)

The "throne of grace" was the mercy seat in the Holiest of Holies, and the book of Hebrews invites us to come on in to witness its glory and to leave our fear at the door. We, in our day, do not realize what an astonishing statement this was in the first century. Under the old covenant Law, people associated God's presence with fear as much they did blessing. Lawbreakers dreaded God's presence because it was a place of wrath. When Christ put away sin, He not only opened God's presence to humanity, He made it a place to be bold.

The images penal substitution offers are striking, but they cannot fully describe Christ's work at Calvary. Penal substitution leaves the cross as something that happened to Christ for us. However, the way Jesus faced evil at the cross is also our example, and we are to overcome evil in the same manner. If we study the history of the early church, after the death of Christ, we will see this is something God's people took to heart in the most extraordinary ways.

The day the Lord died, He exposed the hatred of humanity and then triumphed over it with love. It began in the Garden of Gethsemane. A multitude with swords and clubs came to seize Jesus, and Peter, in his zeal, took a sword and cut off the ear of the High Priest's servant. In Peter's mind, that was the way to overcome—when someone hits you, you hit back. Yet the way of the kingdom of God is to expose darkness with light and to overcome hatred with love. Jesus did not back down from this way even though it would cost Him His life. The High Priest's servant came to destroy Jesus, and for that, he probably deserved to lose more than his ear. Instead, Jesus healed him, because hatred hurts and destroys, and love heals. In restoring the young man's ear, Jesus not only exposed the fellow's evil, He demonstrated the superiority of love. All the hatred in the world could not stop the love of Christ.

Next, Jesus faced His accusers. To be accused wrongly is one of the harder things to bear in life, especially when the label is the exact opposite of who we are. If we love God and someone calls us of the Devil, it hurts badly. Multiply that by infinity to understand what happened to the Lord. He was God in the flesh, yet the religious leaders called Him a blasphemer worthy of death. Never has an accusation been so wrong. To make matters even more unfair, His accusers were *themselves* God's enemies and worthy of death—a contradiction that boggles the mind. And it worsened when the Romans had their turn humiliating Jesus:

> *Then the soldiers led Him away into the hall called Praetorium, and they called together the whole garrison. And they clothed Him with purple; and they twisted a crown of thorns, put it on His head, and began to salute Him, "Hail, King of the Jews!" Then they struck Him on the head with a reed and spat on Him; and bowing the knee, they worshiped Him. And when they had mocked Him, they took the purple off Him, put His own clothes on Him, and led Him out to crucify Him.*
> (MARK 15:16–20)

Caesar claimed to be god and the ruler of the Earth, and those who disagreed ended up on a Roman cross. Jesus was the true King and rightful Ruler of all, however, and human reason screams that mere human beings should not have been allowed to humiliate God. The Lord should have called angels from heaven and shown everyone who was in charge. But if He had, *all would have been lost.* Love alone had to triumph over sin, and *this was love's finest hour.*

In the face of unspeakable injustice, Jesus did not return insult for insult or violence for violence. On the contrary, His words on the cross proved—without a doubt—that God's love was stronger than evil.

> *And when they had come to the place called Calvary, there they crucified Him, and the criminals, one on the right hand and the other on the left. Then Jesus said, "Father, forgive them, for they do not know what they do."* (LUKE 23:33–34)

Love triumphs by not ceasing in the face of evil because love's only defeat is in no longer loving. Dr. Martin Luther King, Jr. said, "I believe that unarmed truth and unconditional love will have the final word in reality. That is why right, temporarily defeated, is stronger than evil triumphant." The more loving the response to evil, the more evil is exposed in contrast. At Calvary, finite humanity spewed forth all the hatred it could muster, and God responded with *infinite love*. The contrast is stunning. This was the hour of love's glory and evil's shame. Yet Christ's work was not complete in merely exposing the darkness; love's final word was yet to come.

The events surrounding Calvary are not just Christ's events; they are our events, too. The scriptures say that Jesus's death and resurrection was our death and resurrection; Paul said, "I have been crucified with Christ...."[5] Likewise, we are raised together with Him into the glory of God.[6] God calls us to participate in and identify with the death and resurrection of Christ just as Jesus identified with and took upon Himself the human condition at the cross. In a sense, *He became us*. His death was the death of all we were so we could partake of who He is.

When we in the twenty-first century think of crucifixion, we think foremost of the pain. Certainly, Christ suffered physical agonies that we cannot begin to imagine. The first-century world thought about it differently, however. Surprisingly, what they dreaded most about the cross was not the pain but *the shame*. Writings from that time speak much more of the shame of crucifixion than its physical torment.[7] In regard to Jesus's ordeal, the book of Hebrews tells us that Jesus "...for the joy that was set before Him, endured the cross, despising the shame...."[8]

The Romans did not invent crucifixion, but they perfected it. When they executed someone on a cross, they had two things in mind. First, they wanted crucifixion to be the most painful death possible. The act of stretching a person out on a cross dislocated the victim's shoulders, and that alone caused immense agony. To further this goal, the soldiers nailed the person's hands and feet to the cross, a torment in itself, but taking a breath required the convicted to raise himself up on the nail holding his feet, causing excruciating torment. And death did not come quickly. Sometimes it took days.

Rome also wanted the cross to be the most shameful death possible. In the movies, we see Jesus on the cross with a loin cloth covering Him. But in reality, the guards stripped their victims bare to cause further indignity. Then, while the person was exposed, humiliated, and defenseless, his enemies would hurl abuse and insults upon him. Such was the fate of Christ.

And those who passed by blasphemed Him, wagging their heads and saying, "You who destroy the temple and build it in three days, save Yourself! If You are the Son of God, come down from the cross."

Likewise the chief priests also, mocking with the scribes and elders, said, "He saved others; Himself He cannot save. If He is the King of Israel, let Him now come down from the cross, and we will believe Him. He trusted in God; let Him deliver Him now if He will have Him; for He said, 'I am the Son of God.'"

Even the robbers who were crucified with Him reviled Him with the same thing. (MATTHEW 27:39–44)

People often say God punished Jesus in our place, focusing on the physical agony of the cross and saying that we deserved that pain. Yet this thought alone cannot express the true depths of redemption. At the cross, *Christ became the human condition.* And we can describe this condition not so much in terms of pain but of *shame and isolation.* Aloneness is the greatest consequence of rejecting God's gift.

When Adam and Eve first rebelled against God, their choice was not to become bad people; their choice was separateness. They broke their tie to God, and in doing so they became self-defined. From that point on, their identity was tied to who they were, what they had, and what they did rather than to God Himself. Then shame and isolation followed. The self-defined man was separated from his neighbor, either because of self-righteousness or because of self-loathing, and because he exalted himself above God, he lost his connection with God as well. Separateness reigned over union and togetherness, and humanity's choice seemed like love's defeat.

At the cross, Jesus not only took our sins upon Himself, *He identified with us fully.* He became the lowest of the low, suffering all the shame and rejection humanity could put upon Him. Even His disciples deserted Him. Though many faithful women stood at the cross with John, the beloved disciple, they could do no more than watch from afar. Perhaps we can begin to imagine such rejection at the hands of men, yet I don't believe any human being can fully comprehend the agony of Jesus's haunting words:

> *Now from the sixth hour until the ninth hour there was darkness over all the land. And about the ninth hour Jesus cried out with a loud voice, saying, "Eli, Eli, lama sabachthani?" that is, "My God, My God, why have You forsaken Me?"* (MATTHEW 27:45–46)

When we think of the power of God, we usually think of His ability to exalt Himself above all others. We all love those "Go, God!" moments in the scriptures when the Lord put the bad guys in their place with a mighty display of power. God, being divine, has the strength to exalt Himself more than any person. But we do not often realize that God also has the ability to lower Himself more than any person. Wonder of wonders, it is this ability that saved us all.

It was a divinely inspired Hebrew concept that one person could represent all. Romans, chapter 5, tells us that Adam's fall was the fall of us all. The second Adam, Jesus Christ, became the self-defined man at the cross. The Bible does not just say that Christ bore our sins; it says that *He became sin in all its fullness.*[9] When Christ died, the self-defined man, in all of his aloneness, died with Him. The cross was our death as much as it was His, and just as humanity participated in Adam's sin, so we participated in the Lord's death.

This is the triumph of God. Through the cross, He snatched self-definition from our hands in a decisive blow against the Tree of the Knowledge of Good and Evil. God Himself tied who we are to Himself once again. What the selfishness of humanity alone could separate only the love of God could put back together.

Now, those who trust in Christ can confidently say that God is in charge of who we are and what we have. Any say we had in the matter Christ took away at the cross; He triumphed over our sins and He triumphed over us. We exalted ourselves, but His humility saved us.

He lowered Himself to nothing so we could have everything. This is the glory of God. All that remains is for us to stand alongside and acknowledge the true King of Kings.

> *And you He made alive, who were dead in trespasses and sins, in which you once walked according to the course of this world, according to the prince of the power of the air, the spirit who now works in the sons of disobedience, among whom also we all once conducted ourselves in the lusts of our flesh, fulfilling the desires of the flesh and of the mind, and were by nature children of wrath, just as the others.*
>
> *But God, who is rich in mercy, because of His great love with which He loved us, even when we were dead in trespasses, made us alive together with Christ (by grace you have been saved), and raised us up together, and made us sit together in the heavenly places in Christ Jesus, that in the ages to come, He might show the exceeding riches of His grace in His kindness toward us in Christ Jesus.* (EPHESIANS 2:1–7)

No passage in the Bible illustrates that God is a God of togetherness better than Ephesians, chapter 2. Christ took upon Himself the sinful condition of humanity and suffered the consequences—He tasted of both physical death and relational death—but these things could not hold Him in their grasp. God raised Him up into the glory of the Father.

But remember: He did not go there alone. Paul uses the word "together" three times in these verses. When Jesus went into the presence of the Father, He took us with Him. Thus, His death was our death, and *together* with Him, His resurrection is our resurrection.

Most Christians make the focus of the resurrection either the past or the future. They consider it an historical event that proves Jesus was who He said He was. Additionally, the resurrection has meaning for life after death. According to the scriptures, we will someday have a body like His after He rose from the grave—one fit for God's heaven.[10] Reading Paul's words in Ephesians, however, his greater emphasis is on relationship, on *the meaning of the resurrection today and every day*. He associates the resurrection with the presence of God. While many Christians also talk about getting closer to God, this talk usually includes the human, *finite* means of getting there: pray more, repent more, do this, don't do that. Meanwhile, God presents His method very clearly: we go there *together with Christ*.

Paul, likewise, takes the relationship approach to the resurrection in Romans, chapter 6. To the apostle, a person touched by the power of the resurrection was *alive* to God.[11] Because of the death and resurrection of Christ, "close to God" is a place we *are*, not a place we are getting to. We share in the resurrected Savior's closeness to the Father. Near to God is our home now, and far from God is a place we never go.

Even so, we still wonder where God is at times. We seem to have little trouble believing we are near to God when our lives are the way we want them to be and we are doing what we think we are supposed to be doing. But what about the day when everything is a mess? What about the day when we are doing everything wrong? It is on those days that we need to look afresh at the empty tomb. The fact that the grave of Christ is still empty means the Lord is intimately near to us on our best day *and* on our worst day. The resurrection was God's triumph over separateness, and we are to participate in His triumph *every* day, never diminishing it.

Additionally, Ephesians, chapter 2, tells us that the death and resurrection of Christ is the way to God's kindness. Notice the progression: Paul says that we were formerly children of wrath, but the child of wrath is no more. Sometimes, we try to bring this child back to life by thinking God has forsaken us. Yet the sacrifice of Christ reminds us that wrath's demise is as certain as the cross.

According to Paul, participation in Christ takes us to a kindness so great that we can't experience it all in this life; it will take the ages to come for God to reveal it all. In other words, it is infinite. Do we think we know how good God is? The empty tomb says there is more and *there will always be more*.

The death and resurrection of Christ totally changed the dynamics of walking with God. Under the new covenant, the emphasis changed from our works to the Christ's finished work. We still have work to do in the Kingdom of God, but much of that work is in *changing our minds*. Our perspective must change from getting there to being there, from doing to being, and from working to resting.

As Paul said, God wants us to live "in Christ." And to do this, we must understand how much Jesus identified with us. Anything that kept us from God died with Christ at the cross. Christ did not just take away our sins; He died to give us a new identity—one that is tied to Him. God wants us to see something infinitely beloved and infinitely blessed when we look at ourselves because that's *exactly* what He sees when He looks at us. The love of Christ is truth and reality. Not living in Christ is to live a false life.

This is why overcoming in the new covenant has to do more with seeing than doing. The overcomer is the one who looks intently at Jesus then changes his opinion of himself accordingly. The overcomer is the one who knows that Christ's overcoming is all that matters. For the Lord won a great triumph at the cross: He triumphed over all that we were and all that we did that we might live in who He is and what He has done.

The day God rolled the stone away was the victory of the gift; we cannot stop it any more than we can put Christ back in the grave. And so, the gift will reign forever in our lives, the infinite in the finite. (God gives the gift of Himself relentlessly.)

— 8 —

The Meaning of the Rent Veil

And Jesus cried out with a loud voice, and breathed His last.
Then the veil of the temple was torn in two from top to bottom.
(MARK 15:37–38)

When Jesus uttered His last words while dying on the cross, God tore the veil in the Temple from top to bottom. It is one of the most powerful images in the entire Bible; with this act, God told the world that everything had changed. Humanity's relationship with Him would never be the same, nor would our relationships with each other.

To help us understand the power of what God did, let us take a little walk through the Jewish Temple of Jesus's day. The first king Herod, Herod the Great, claimed to be king of the Jews. He knew the Jewish people judged their kings by their king's relationship with the Temple.[1] This idea went back to the days of David and Solomon, when David planned the original Temple and Solomon built it. Hezekiah and Josiah, who were considered good kings, cleansed the Temple from pagan influences. Zerubbabel rebuilt it after the Babylonians destroyed it. Later, Judas Maccabaeus cleansed it again at the Maccabean revolt. Today's Jews still commemorate Judas

Maccabaeus's great victory and all the miracles that accompanied it at the celebration known as Hanukkah.

Wanting to win the people's hearts, King Herod decided to build the grandest temple of them all. Ever since the Babylonians destroyed the Temple in 587 BC, the Jewish house of God had not regained the glory of Solomon's Temple. Herod took all the measurements of the original and doubled them, thinking the people would surely respond to a temple twice as glorious as Solomon's.

And indeed it was. Solomon's Temple took seven years to complete; Herod's took eighty-two.[2] In fact, the Herod who started it was not the Herod who finished it. Agrippa II, Herod the Great's great-grandson, was king when the Jews completed God's House.

We have some pretty big church buildings in the modern era, yet none of them compares to Herod's Temple. The Temple complex, with its adjoining structures, was so big that it took up as much as 20 percent of Jerusalem.[3] Its floors were marble, and its walls were white limestone, which gave its buildings a glowing appearance. Many of its interior walls were covered in solid gold, its tapestries rivaled any in the world, and its gates were so huge it took twenty or thirty men to open and close them. It was said in that day that a person had never truly seen a beautiful building unless he had seen Herod's Temple.

In some of our large churches today, we might have fifty or more ministers serving a congregation, but *thousands* of priests and Levites served the Temple in Jerusalem. The daily operations of the Jewish House of God were a sight to behold, and the great feasts there were even more of a spectacle when thousands of worshippers flocked to Jerusalem to participate. Without a doubt, the Temple in Jerusalem was the center of Jewish religious life.

Despite its beauty and grand presentations, Herod's Temple said something about the people's relationship with God and with each other. If we had to pick one word to describe the Temple's message about the nature of relationships before Christ, a good choice would be "separation." There was separation between God and humanity, between man and man, and even between woman and man.

The Temple had three major courts or divisions.[4] The outermost area was called the Court of the Gentiles and was a space reserved primarily for tourists and Gentiles who came to honor Israel's God. People came from all over the world to see Herod's glorious Temple, and as long as they were respectful, the Jews allowed them to behold the majesty of God's most holy building. Foreigners could also purchase various animals for the priests to offer as a sacrifice, though they had to use the Temple's own holy currency. And that required the assistance of money changers, who were notorious for giving very unfair exchange rates. It was because of these money changers that Jesus said the Temple had become a "den of thieves."[5]

At the entrance to the second court, a large sign spelled out an ominous warning in bright red letters. Not too long ago, archeologists discovered fragments of the original engraving. It said:

> No foreigner is to enter within the forecourt and the balustrade around the sanctuary. Whoever is caught will have himself to blame for his subsequent death.[6]

Those who were not descendants of Abraham, who were uncircumcised, who were unclean, or who did not keep Torah could not enter the second court. It was more holy than the first court, and a worshipper had to follow suit to cross the divide. But Gentiles were not the only ones barred from this second area. The lame, the blind, lepers, and notorious sinners such as the tax collectors could not enter either.

In other words, if a person's lineage was not right or if what a person did was not right, he or she could not worship with the righteous. And if someone unclean or unholy did manage to enter the forbidden area, it could cost him his life. The Romans did not allow the Jews to carry out capital punishment except in instances of this one offense.

The second court, or center court, was divided into three sub-courts. The Court of the Women was first, and as the name implies, Jewish women could worship here (as could Jewish men and children). Beyond that was the Court of Israel, and only Jewish laymen could enter here. Finally, there was the Court of the Priesthood. This area was the closest to the Holiest of Holies, and a person had to have the high calling of a priest to enter a place so near to God.

Beyond the second court was the Holiest of Holies, or God's court. While the Temple provided the Gentiles with their own court and the Jews with another, the third court was God's dwelling alone. A thick veil surrounded this most holy place, and beyond the veil was the *Shekinah*—the outshining of the glory of God Himself. The Jews considered the Holiest of Holies to be the place where heaven touched and became one with the Earth. No one except the High Priest could enter the Holiest of Holies, and he only did so once a year, at the Feast of Atonement. If a Gentile went into the Court of the Jews, man would kill him. However, if a person went into the Holiest of Holies unlawfully, the Old Testament tells us God would kill him.

It is interesting that the Torah had no command to stone Gentiles who came too near to the Holiest of Holies, nor did it contain many of the other distinctions instituted by the religious authorities in Herod's Temple. But one has only to look at the Holiest of Holies to see why the Jews added them. If we tend to act like our concept of God, and if the Lord excludes those who are less holy than Himself, we will naturally exclude those we consider less holy than us.

Before Christ came, the Temple was a picture of God's relationship with humanity and of humanity's relationships among its members. There was separation between God and humanity, Jew and Gentile, and even man and woman. Self-righteousness leaves us looking down on our neighbor and up to an unreachable God, and such was the case in the culture that built Herod's Temple. By dying and rising from the grave, Jesus tore down these walls of separation—tore right through the veil of *Shekinah*—to flood the Earth with heaven and bring back those "who once were far off."

Therefore, remember that you, once Gentiles in the flesh—who are called Uncircumcision by what is called the Circumcision made in the flesh by hands—that at that time you were without Christ, being aliens from the commonwealth of Israel and strangers from the covenants of promise, having no hope and without God in the world. But now in Christ Jesus you who once were far off have been brought near by the blood of Christ.

For He Himself is our peace, who has made both one, and has broken down the middle wall of separation.... (EPHESIANS 2:11–14)

Now, therefore, you are no longer strangers and foreigners, but fellow citizens with the saints and members of the household of God.... (EPHESIANS 2:19)

What "middle wall" was Paul talking about in Ephesians 2:14? No doubt, he was talking about the wall between the Court of the Gentiles and the second courts of the Jews. In Ephesians 2:19, the apostle tells the Gentiles they are no longer foreigners. Recall that forboding sign between the Court of the Jews and the Court of the Gentiles: "No foreigner is to enter within the forecourt and the balustrade around the sanctuary...." When Jesus died for all, that sign had to go. There was no longer any distinction between Jew and Gentile; God made them into *one new person.*

For you are all sons of God through faith in Christ Jesus. For as many of you as were baptized into Christ have put on Christ. There is neither Jew nor Greek, there is neither slave nor free, there is neither male nor female; for you are all one in Christ Jesus. (GALATIANS 3:26–28)

Paul shows us that God removed the separations of the middle court as well. For instance, there is no longer a distinction between male and female when it comes to one's closeness to God. This does not mean there is no more gender, but in Jesus's day, people considered men more righteous than women.[7] Men generally did not talk to women in public, and education in theological matters was for men only.

Today, we don't realize how radical Jesus was in these matters. He gave women the respectful title of "Daughters of Abraham,"[8] not only talking with them in public but allowing them to be His disciples as well.[9] In the book of Luke, we read the account of Jesus's stay at the home of Mary and Martha. Mary was sitting at the feet of Jesus, listening to the Lord teach, and Martha got upset because Mary was not helping with the meal preparations. Jesus told Martha that Mary had chosen the better thing, however. Not knowing the customs of the day, we might wonder why Luke recorded such a seemingly trivial incident. Yet at that time, it served to show that the kingdom of God was near. A woman was sitting at the feet of a rabbi, a place reserved for men, learning about the kingdom of God. This is yet more evidence that Jesus was a rabbi like no other. He tore down the wall between the Court of the Women and the Court of Israel in His ministry, and He removed this distinction in all finality at the cross.

But you are a chosen generation, a royal priesthood, a holy nation, His own special people, that you may proclaim the praises of Him who called you out of darkness into His marvelous light.... (1 PETER 2:9)

Another wall that would crumble at the cross was the one between the priesthood and the other courts. According to the Torah, the descendants of Aaron would serve as priests, members of the tribe of Levi would offer assistance, and only these men could go to God on behalf of everyone else.[10] Those not of this lineage could not offer sacrifices to the Lord themselves lest they be punished with certain death; all others had to go through the Temple priesthood. Now, under the new covenant, we see a holy nation where all are priests unto God.[11] *All* may approach the throne of grace.

We still sometimes try to put up the wall between the priesthood and the laity in our day. Are clergy really closer to God than the laity? Does the Lord more readily hear their prayers? Are they more holy or righteous? To think so is to give insult to the cross. God tore down that wall a long time ago.

Seeing then that we have a great High Priest who has passed through the heavens, Jesus the Son of God, let us hold fast our confession. For we do not have a High Priest who cannot sympathize with our weaknesses, but was in all points tempted as we are, yet without sin. Let us therefore come boldly to the throne of grace, that we may obtain mercy and find grace to help in time of need. (HEBREWS 4:14–16)

As we discussed in chapter 7, what this passage contains is a little Temple talk about the walls and the veil. The throne of grace was the mercy seat in the Holiest of Holies, and because of our High Priest, the Lord Jesus, we can now come into the presence of God without fear. The veil between God and humanity has been forever removed.

Under the old covenant, no one came into God's presence boldly. During the Jewish Feast of Atonement, for example, only the High Priest entered beyond the veil to make an offering for the people. We might think the High Priest would be overjoyed on the day he could enter into the *Shekinah* of God; on the contrary, fear ruled that time. Imagine the pressure the High Priest faced as he went through the exacting rituals the Law demanded—the fate of Israel for the coming year depended on his performance. One error could mean disaster, not only for him but for the whole nation.

Fortunately, Jesus, the Highest Priest of all, accomplished His mission, and God accepted the His sacrifice. Now the presence of God is available forever, a place of love and mercy, not condemnation.

For He made Him who knew no sin to be sin for us, that we might become the righteousness of God in Him.
(2 CORINTHIANS 5:21)

The various courts and sub-courts of the Temple reflected levels of righteousness. A person had to have the righteousness of a Gentile to enter the first court. (In other words, not much!) A worshipper with the righteousness of a devout Jew could enter the second court, which meant he or she was a descendant of Abraham and kept God's

Law. But within this second court, worthiness was further divided: if a person had the righteousness of a Jewish woman, he or she could enter the Court of the Women; if this fellow had the righteousness of a Jewish man, he could proceed into the Court of Israel; and if his righteousness was even greater than that of a layman, based on an even more exclusive lineage, he could enter the Court of the Priesthood. According to the Torah, priests had to be the descendants of Aaron, and they had to keep more exacting laws and rituals. And since *no one* had righteousness as great as God's, even God had His own court.

God in Christ Jesus removed all the distinctions of the Temple by *becoming sin for all* and by *giving His own righteousness to all*. In the old system, a person's lineage, occupation, and character meant everything. Under the new covenant, God took the righteousness issue out of humanity's hands once and for all.

When God gave His own righteousness as a gift, the veil that had stood for 1500 years proved no match for this immense love. We cannot comprehend the divine satisfaction the Lord must have experienced as He forcefully ripped the veil from top to bottom. Now, *nothing* could separate Him from His beloved.

With the fall of the wall between God and man, the walls between our neighbors and ourselves fell also. If both Jew and Gentile have the righteousness of God, can there be any distinction between the two? If men and women have the righteousness of Christ, how can one gender look down upon the other? If both the priesthood and the laity have the righteousness of Christ, how can one claim to be closer to God than the other? In dying and rising from the grave, *Jesus made peace in every human relationship.* The self-righteousness of the old order led to separation, and the new covenant gift of righteousness leads to union. When God became one with us through Christ, we became one with each other.

The Jewish people expected their Messiah/King to build the true temple of God. However, their King did this in an unexpected way: He built it not out of earthly stone but out of *living* stone. *His people would be the new covenant temple of the Holy Spirit.*[12] The place where heaven touches Earth is no longer a building in Jerusalem; it is God's people. In fact, His beloved see God's house every time they look in the mirror.

The whole world changed the day Jesus rose from the dead, and it is no wonder Jesus prophesied that the old covenant Temple's days were numbered. In Matthew 24, Jesus pointed to Herod's Temple and said it would be thrown down "with not one stone...left...upon another,"[13] and His words came to pass. Only seven years after the Temple was completed, the Romans destroyed it. In the great fire that engulfed the structure, the Temple's vast quantities of gold melted, and to recover it all, the Romans tore down each and every stone.[14]

The torn veil is a reminder of God's triumph, and we must be humble in this fact. But human arrogance takes many forms. One is to believe closeness to God is our achievement. Another is to believe our weaknesses and failures can undo what God has done. Contempt for our brother and "us" and "them" thinking also violates the new covenant. God made it clear that humanity could not take down the veil, and it is just as clear that we cannot put it back up. Instead, we must open our eyes not only to how much God loves us but also to how much He loves our neighbor. "I am closer to God than you" is a human-made distinction ripped in two just as assuredly as the veil itself.

In Jesus's day, some welcomed God's gift of unbridled love and some opposed it. The latter preferred that the walls of separation remain, and these same people would go on to oppose grace's coming champion, the Apostle Paul, in a great clash over the meaning and purpose of the Law. Though God tore the veil in Herod's Temple, a veil remained over the eyes of some people—those who rejected the gift. And their rejection was similar to the conflict that raged against Jesus, but in a different framework. It is to Paul's day and message that we now turn.

Paul and the Law

If we are going to live in God's gift, we must understand our relationship to God's Law and its purpose. The problem with the Law is that it seems incompatible with grace. Some say God's love comes with no strings attached—His blessings are free and His mercy is infinite. Therefore, our behavior has no bearing on our standing with God. Others say there have to be strings. If we rid ourselves of God's commandments, the result will be lawlessness. If there is no reward for doing good and abundant mercy when we do evil, people will do whatever they want. This view recognizes that, at times, we humans want to do evil more than we want to do good. And it concludes that we need a well-defined system of right and wrong and a clear system of rewards and punishments to go with it.

This conflict between justice and mercy is emotionally charged. People take sides and fiercely defend their opinions. One side has their grace Bible verses and the other has their obedience Bible verses, and the two rarely meet.

Whatever our view on the tension between Law and grace, our champion is most likely the Apostle Paul, who seems to come down on both sides of the issue. No one proclaimed the grace of God like Paul, but at the same time, he painted a detailed picture of how Christians should behave. It is difficult to determine if the great apostle was a

Torah lover or a Torah hater. While among the Jews, he behaved like a Jew. For example, he circumcised his young disciple, Timothy.[1] Yet when a group of Judiazers was trying to persuade the Gentile church at Galatia to embrace circumcision, Paul said he wished they would "cut themselves off."[2] It does not take a vivid imagination to know what he was talking about.

Paul gave his congregations commandments that covered everything from family life to interaction with human governments. In Romans, chapter 7, Paul proclaimed that the Law was a good thing. Yet at the same time, he said that if believers did not die to the Law, they could not have a relationship with God.

Well, which is it, Paul? Are we better off without the Law, or is the Law a good thing that plays a role in our walk with God? The scriptures seem to say both. Undoubtedly, when the Bible appears to contradict itself, the best course is not to take sides but to *ask why both sides are true*. Seeking to understand how seemingly incompatible ideas can live together is a harder road to take, but it is the only one that leads to satisfaction. Surprisingly, Paul, the one who appeared two-faced on the Law, is the perfect man to guide us on our journey.

> *Therefore the law was our tutor to bring us to Christ, that we might be justified by faith. But after faith has come, we are no longer under a tutor.* (GALATIANS 3:24–25)

Many people in Paul's day looked at God's commandments merely as do's and don'ts, seeing them as God's means of deciding who was a good person and who was a bad person. They thought the Law was a strict order to "Behave!" but Paul had a much deeper understanding of Torah. To him, its end was not to guide us in putting on a good show for God; its purpose was Christ. God did not give His commands so we could say, "Look at me! I am doing a great job, Lord!" Neither did God give His laws to make us hide in shame when we are not doing well. And He especially did not reveal His ordinances so we could count ourselves superior to our brother.

For Paul, the Law was a guide that pointed to Christ, not to us. In the apostle's time, the new covenant was coming into fullness, and God was calling His people to an exodus every bit as real as the one in Moses's day. This time, however, it was an exodus of the heart, and the people's relationship with Torah was changing. They were finding that Torah was no longer about their own faithfulness; in fact, true obedience to the Law meant leaving trust in their own faithfulness for utter dependence on the faithfulness of Christ. Those reading the Torah with the help of the Holy Spirit focused on Christ rather than on their own successes and failures.

Do not think that I came to destroy the Law or the Prophets. I did not come to destroy but to fulfill. (MATTHEW 5:17)

For 1500 years, before Christ came, the Jews had the Torah—the first five books of our modern Bible. And obeying Torah was not just observing the Ten Commandments; the Law also told the Jews how and when to worship God through sacrifices and Israel's great feasts. It taught them how to be holy through circumcision and about the idea of clean and unclean, and it contained the story of God's chosen people. Israel's forefathers' obedience and disobedience was an example for all, and keeping their stories close to one's heart was part of keeping Torah.

Through Jesus and the apostles that followed, God began to reveal that Torah was about far more than the Jews and what God required of them; it was about Christ. In fact, *it pointed to Him on every page.* Paul said that all the old covenant ordinances and many of the Old Testament stories were foreshadows of Christ; what he was teaching was nothing new, as these truths that were once hidden in the Law and the prophets were now revealed through the Holy Spirit. In 2 Corinthians, chapter 3, the Apostle Paul said just as Moses "put a veil over his face," so there was a veil over the Old Testament and its full glory. When the Lord removed that covering, what God's beloved saw was Christ (2 Corinthians 3:13–18).

The Old Testament is filled with physical representations of the spiritual realities of Christ. And it is interesting that God said the historical events and the things people could see with their eyes were only the shadow. *Unseen things, or spiritual matters, were the substance.*

In Galatians, chapter 4, Paul tells us that the story of Abraham's sons, Ishmael and Isaac, goes beyond an historical account. It was the story of two covenants: one based on the effort of man, the other on the effort of God. God said that Sarah, Abraham's wife, would bear a son, but when Sarah and Abraham grew tired of waiting for God to fulfill His word, they turned to Hagar, an Egyptian maidservant. She bore Abraham the son we know as Ishmael, and Paul says that Ishmael was born after the flesh, according to man's potential and not according to the Lord's faithfulness. Ishmael is a picture of the old covenant, which was based on the efforts of man. In contrast, Isaac was a miracle baby, born beyond the possibility of man and according to the promise of God. He foreshadowed the new covenant, which centers on the efforts of God.

Other biblical stories also speak of the two covenants. Paul hints in Romans, chapter 9, that the tale of Jacob and Esau also foretold of things to come. Jacob, the younger brother, represented the younger, new covenant, and Esau the old covenant. It was the younger who found favor with God, and likewise, it is the new creation that enjoys God's pleasure. The old finds His displeasure.

Many people think Paul wrote the book of Hebrews, where we read that Moses, the central figure of the Torah, was himself a type of Christ. Moses gave God's people the Law through the old covenant; Jesus gave God's people grace and truth through the new covenant. 1 Corinthians, chapter 10, tells us that when the children of Israel crossed the Red Sea, they were baptized into Moses; in the new covenant, we are baptized into Christ. And the rock Moses struck in the wilderness pointed to a spiritual Rock—Jesus—from whom would come living waters.

Though the shadow was glorious, the substance, which is Christ, far outshines the glory of the old. Israel's old covenant stories weren't just about its past; its great leaders, deliverers, and prophets were all *types* of Christ. They symbolically pointed ahead to their coming Messiah. Jesus, in a sense, fulfilled the story of Israel.

*So let no one judge you in food or in drink, or regarding a
festival or a new moon or sabbaths, which are a shadow of
things to come, but the substance is of Christ.*
(COLOSSIANS 2:16–17)

Jewish worship, with all its ceremony, also pointed to Christ. For
instance, one of the three major feasts of Israel was Passover. Every
year, a representative from every family traveled to Jerusalem with
a blemish-free Passover lamb, taking his offering to the Temple to
shed its blood in sacrifice. A priest would then take the blood of the
lamb and sprinkle it on the altar. We can only imagine the spectacle
as thousands of worshippers came to participate in one of God's
most holy celebrations.

The Lord did not ordain this ritual so His people could boast in
what they did for Him, however. He never wanted His people to walk
away from the Passover feast thinking they had done something to get
in good with God for another year, nor did He want His worshippers
to think they were better than those who did not keep the feast.
People who thought keeping the Passover made them superior
completely missed its message. The Passover lamb did not point to
the works of humanity but to the works of Christ, the one who would
take away the sins of the world and bring grace to all. God intended
for His people to get their eyes off of who they were and what they
had done and look at His mercy instead; Paul said that Christ is "our
Passover."[3] The Passover feast was *a living image of God's sacrifice*,
and God wanted it to make His people more merciful, not more
exclusive.[4]

Passover was the first of seven feasts mandated by the Torah, and
all seven point to Christ. For many generations, God was preparing
His people to receive their Messiah. But as Paul testified, when it was
time for the new covenant to swallow up the old, many refused to let
go of the shadow for the substance.

Even the Torah's ordinances such as Sabbath keeping found
fulfillment in Christ. When the Law told the Jews to keep the day
of rest, God was very serious about not working on His holy day.
The penalty for breaking the Sabbath was death because the Lord

was speaking to His people about something more important than taking off some time every week. Though the voice of Moses said the Sabbath was about physical work, the voice of Christ said the Sabbath was about something far greater: it was a call for God's people to enter *God's rest.* It was beckoning all who would listen to cease working in order to enter into God's blessing and to trust in the finished work of the Christ. The Lord did the work of bringing the people into His glory, and the people's job was to rest in what He had done.

Old covenant Sabbath keeping was a picture of the new covenant relationship with God. Just as physical labor was a violation to the old covenant Sabbath, so is making God's presence anything but a gift in the new covenant. The old rest concerned the body; the fulfillment concerns the heart.

Similarly, the Torah's circumcision and purity laws were foreshadows of the things of Christ. Removing the male foreskin set apart the Jews, and the things Jews could not touch or eat made them different from the other nations of the Earth. Yet these are physical things. What would set apart the new creation would be spiritual. Paul spoke of the circumcision of the heart, and just as the Jews removed flesh from the body, so must Christians set aside the previous life of independence from God. The old way constituted the realm of the flesh, and in Paul's mind, it was purity that mattered. To go back into the righteousness of the old covenant was to be impure; it was forsaking the gift.

We might conclude that Jesus fulfilled the story of Israel as well as its ceremonial laws, such as Sabbath keeping, circumcision, and the great feasts, but surely we must still fulfill God's moral Law. Though Christ has come, we remain obligated to keep the commandments, such as "You shall not murder" or "You shall not steal," right? It is true that Christ did not come to make a world where anything goes, but even obedience finds a new focus under the new covenant. The source of holiness is no longer living by certain rules but maintaining *a living relationship with the Lord.* Under the old covenant, God gave commands to make His people holy; under the new covenant, He gives us a Person—the Person of Jesus Christ.

Now the works of the flesh are evident, which are: adultery, fornication, uncleanness, lewdness, idolatry, sorcery, hatred, contentions, jealousies, outbursts of wrath, selfish ambitions, dissensions, heresies, envy, murders, drunkenness, revelries, and the like; of which I tell you beforehand, just as I also told you in time past, that those who practice such things will not inherit the kingdom of God.

But the fruit of the Spirit is love, joy, peace, longsuffering, kindness, goodness, faithfulness, gentleness, self-control. Against such there is no law. (GALATIANS 5:19–23)

We often read the deeds of the flesh and the spirit as if they were a mere list of things we are to do and not do. To Paul, however, this passage is not a description of good and evil; it is a picture of a life that is connected to God and one that is not. Further, the topic is not good behavior and bad behavior; it is the Law versus grace. Paul's term "the flesh" is closely tied to the old covenant and captures the realm—the limitations—of human potential. The self-righteousness of the old covenant trapped humanity in disconnect with God and thus in the deeds of the flesh.

Paul likewise ties the spirit to the new covenant. In this new economy, where righteousness is a gift and God is a gift, good behavior is also a gift. It comes from participation in the gift of Christ. Therefore, we see that Paul's discourse about the deeds of the flesh and the fruit of the spirit is more about relationship that it is about right and wrong behavior. It is not even about things to strive for or things to strive against; it is a picture of separateness and its consequences and union and its fruit.

But if the ministry of death, written and engraved on stones, was glorious, so that the children of Israel could not look steadily at the face of Moses because of the glory of his countenance, which glory was passing away, how will the ministry of the Spirit not be more glorious? For if the ministry of condemnation had glory, the ministry of righteousness exceeds much more in glory. (2 CORINTHIANS 3:7–9)

The Law points to Christ, but it points at us *first*—so that it might lead us to Christ. The Law has the ministry of death and condemnation. God did not give the Law to make us feel good about ourselves. Nor did God give it to be a way to earn His approval. Rather, the Law reveals how much we need a Savior, and this function is yet another way the Law is our tutor.

When old-time revivalists preached, they often began with what they called their "Law Work,"[5] using the Law as a measuring stick for seeing how far people fell short of the glory of God. The evangelists would sometimes spend a day or two talking about God's standard without even mentioning Christ. In their message, the Law revealed to people's hearts how much they fell short of God's glory, and God's commands measured how much people fell short of God's righteousness. Then, when the Law had done its ministry of condemnation, these old-time preachers would hold up the grace of the new covenant, and people would come running to Christ.

The Law does more than define sin; it is a ruler in a system that isolates us from God by its very nature. As Paul said in Romans, chapter 7, "...the Law is holy, and the commandment holy and just and good," but the commandment alone can only lead to spiritual death. Even if a person tries to keep Torah with all of his strength, all he is doing is building a righteousness of his own—and thus, a disconnect from God. God gave the Law to contain humanity in a flawed system of its own making, where separation from God reigned because of condemnation and egocentric self-righteousness. It is no wonder Paul, when speaking of the old covenant relationship to the Law, cried out, "Who will deliver me from this body of death?"[6] The only solution is to leave the old system behind and become something new.

The new covenant man is joined with Christ. When the old covenant man was shut up in separateness and isolation, looking only to himself to find his identity, the Law was the mirror God handed him. Under grace, humanity has a new mirror—the love and union of Jesus Christ.

This way of finding out who we are by looking at Christ was a continual theme in Paul's writings. In a world dominated by Caesar and paganism, there were so many things competing to define the early church. These powers called God's people insignificant and weak, and the old covenant Law—commandments that were literally written in stone—said God's people, especially the Gentiles, were unworthy of God's presence. Yet Paul labored so the church might see Christ had conquered all these powers. The Lord now reigned over all, and the church reigned with Him. And as direct reflections of Christ Himself, God's beloved needed to embrace the title "holy," because refusing to do so would be to fall back in the old system that was passing away.

> *For we are the circumcision, who worship God in the Spirit, rejoice in Christ Jesus, and have no confidence in the flesh, though I also might have confidence in the flesh. If anyone else thinks he may have confidence in the flesh, I more so: circumcised the eighth day, of the stock of Israel, of the tribe of Benjamin, a Hebrew of the Hebrews; concerning the law, a Pharisee; concerning zeal, persecuting the church; concerning the righteousness which is in the law, blameless.*
>
> *But what things were gain to me, these I have counted loss for Christ. Yet indeed I also count all things loss for the excellence of the knowledge of Christ Jesus my Lord, for whom I have suffered the loss of all things, and count them as rubbish, that I may gain Christ and be found in Him, not having my own righteousness, which is from the law, but that which is through faith in Christ, the righteousness which is from God by faith....*
> (PHILIPPIANS 3:3–9)

When we think of coming to Christ, we usually think of turning from being a bad person to being a good person. We love testimonies of people who turned from terrible sins to follow Christ. People write books and give great speeches about how Jesus freed them from their addictions or turned their hearts from wrongdoing. But when was the last time we heard a story like Paul's? He proclaimed that Christ freed him from his own righteousness.

Jesus said, "If anyone desires to come after Me, let him deny himself, and take up his cross daily, and follow Me."[7] Paul's story reveals that Jesus was talking about something much deeper than turning from our bad habits. If self-denial were just a matter of "being good," the Pharisees would have been the champions of the kingdom of God. Taking up one's cross meant letting go of *anything* a person held onto that kept him from living in the gift of Christ. Paul had to put aside his own righteousness to live in the righteousness of Christ, and to him, as we read above, this was a loss so great that he called it "the loss of all things."

According to Paul's message, *true obedience* to the Law meant coming to Christ. This is what the Torah was saying in its shadows and commandments alike. Paul spoke further of those who disobeyed the Law in Romans, chapter 10.

> *For I bear them witness that they have a zeal for God, but not according to knowledge. For they being ignorant of God's righteousness, and seeking to establish their own righteousness, have not submitted to the righteousness of God. For Christ is the end of the law for righteousness to everyone who believes.*
> (ROMANS 10:2–4)

Paul's greatest enemies were the Judiazers, fellows who had the same nature as those who persecuted Jesus.[8] They had great zeal for Torah, but they did not understand what it was saying. The Law was telling the people to come to Christ and leave their own righteousness behind, but Paul's enemies still believed the Gentiles had to keep the Torah's ordinances (such as circumcision) to be right with God. Many of them had one foot in the old covenant and one foot in the new, similar to the disobedient Hebrews in the day of Moses who wanted to go back to Egypt.

The people who opposed Christ and Paul help us understand the nature of new covenant obedience. If all we do is keep certain do's and don'ts, we have not yet obeyed—joined with—God. Obedience is coming to Christ; it is *living in the gift of God.* That is why men like the Pharisees and the Judiazers could be perfect according to the letter of the Law but still be grossly disobedient.

Paul was very much a man of the Law, yet the apostle was a champion *of the spirit*, not of the letter. To this hero of the new covenant, Torah was exceedingly good because it led to Christ. Astonishingly, in order to fully obey the Law, God's people had to leave it, the old covenant, behind and make the journey into the glorious new covenant. Torah was leading Israel, not just to a land of promise but straight into the presence of God through Christ.

We do not have quite the same journey today as the first-century Jews, as we are not coming out of the old covenant like they were. The essence of our exodus is the same, however: we are still required to forsake our own righteousness, whether we have a little or a lot, for the gift of God. It is the only way to make our home in the promise of God's grace.

10

Dead to the Law?

Or do you not know, brethren (for I speak to those who know the law), that the law has dominion over a man as long as he lives? For the woman who has a husband is bound by the law to her husband as long as he lives. But if the husband dies, she is released from the law of her husband. So then if, while her husband lives, she marries another man, she will be called an adulteress; but if her husband dies, she is free from that law, so that she is no adulteress, though she has married another man. Therefore, my brethren, you also have become dead to the law through the body of Christ, that you may be married to another—to Him who was raised from the dead, that we should bear fruit to God. For when we were in the flesh, the sinful passions which were aroused by the law were at work in our members to bear fruit to death. But now we have been delivered from the law, having died to what we were held by, so that we should serve in the newness of the Spirit and not in the oldness of the letter. (ROMANS 7:1–6)

Years ago, I did a presentation on the Internet called "Dead to the Law," and I have never gotten such a negative response to anything I have ever taught. Some people said they never wanted to hear from me again. "How could a preacher possibly be against God's Law?" was one response. "Christians are fighting for the right to display the Ten Commandments in public, and you are bashing God's standard!" Well, I did not say I was against the Ten Commandments, and I never said the Law was a bad thing, but we do have to *die to it*—redirect our life instead to Christ—if we are going to have a relationship with God.

In Romans, chapter 7, Paul says that the Law is a good thing. As we saw earlier, the commandments are a reflection of God's character, revealing His concern for our well-being. Yet the apostle also tells us that God's commandments are against us, contrary to us, and even hostile toward us.[1]

To help us understand how something so good can be hostile, let us look at an example from modern life. On our roads, there are speed limits and punishments for breaking them. Speed limit signs define who is a speeder and who is not, and as long as we stay under the limit, we will have no problem with the law. However, if we drive too fast, the law of the land can become hostile toward us. It will pinpoint us as a lawbreaker and then dictate our punishment. We might get a ticket! And if our violation is severe enough, the state might judge us unworthy of being a free citizen, sending us to prison. Overall, these laws are considered good because they protect us from doing harm to ourselves and to others.

If we look at the old covenant Law, we will see it is similar. It defines the kind of righteousness we need to receive God's approval. And since the Law is a reflection of God's character, it says we need righteousness on par with God's. The Law also sets the punishment for falling short of the glory of God. In Paul's words, "the wages of sin is death" (Romans 6:23), and under the Law, if we do not deserve God, we cannot have Him.

Such a measure would be fine for us if we were actually able to meet God's requirement. No matter what we do, however, we will fall short, and the Law will come against us. It will define us as unworthy and dole out its punishment, which is to be without God.

The Law proves the point that *no one deserves God*, but it also leads us to wonder why the Lord would set such an impossible standard. Some say the Law's message is that we human beings are pitiful and worthless compared to the Lord. Yet if this is the whole point of the Law, its end can only be isolation from God. Therefore, the Law must have a deeper purpose, and that is to drive us to grace— to union with God rather than separation. It is designed to lead us to the conclusion that the only way we can have righteousness on par with God's is if He gives us His own righteousness as a gift.

Paul said that the Law aroused sinful passions, possibly meaning that being told not to do something makes one want to do sinful things all the more. However, humanity's predicament under the Law was even worse than that. God's commandments not only defined sin, they accentuated humanity's self-righteousness. If there were no Law, there would have been no Pharisees. The Law, combined with humanity's ignorance, made people strive to have righteousness as great as God's. Born of ignorance and strengthened by pride, such striving easily led people away from union with Christ.

It is no wonder Paul said that being under the Law was like being trapped. It held people in a system that either shone a spotlight on their shortcomings or inflated their egos, increasing the distance between the Lord and His beloved even further.

This calamity may sound a little familiar. (Remember chapter 2?) A long time ago, Adam made that fateful choice to partake of forbidden fruit that represented independence from God. The tree that bore this fruit was called the Tree of the Knowledge of Good and Evil, and as the name implies, there were two sides to its fruit: one was self-righteousness, or humanity's attempt to be as great as God; the other was not only evil but the knowledge that we do not measure up. The Law, though it was good, now accentuated humanity's condition in plain, visible, even arousing terms.

From that point on, there was no way out. We needed a Savior who would provide a way to escape. And it was Jesus who answered the call, delivering us from our independence through the cross.

For I through the law died to the Law that I might live to God. I have been crucified with Christ; it is no longer I who live, but Christ lives in me; and the life [that] I now live in the flesh I live by faith in the Son of God, who loved me and gave Himself for me. (GALATIANS 2:19–20)

Many people take Galatians 2:20 out of its context, saying it means that I, the bad person, died with Christ so the Lord, who is good, could live through me. While there is truth to this viewpoint, it fails to provide the complete picture of this passage. The topic of the book of Galatians is the Law, and Paul does not deviate from this subject. The death he is talking about here is to the Law.

Recall Paul's own testimony in the book of Philippians. His journey was not going from being a bad person to being a good person; it was going from his own righteousness to the righteousness of Christ. The means of his journey was the cross, and through it, *he died to his own righteousness* so that he could live in the righteousness of Christ.

The apostle was born into a covenant based upon the Law. It was a system that trapped him and, by its very nature, kept him from God. As long as he tried to stand alone before God, he could not *have* God.

The solution God provided was so astonishing it boggles the mind. The only way Paul could get to the Lord was *to die to his efforts to reach Him.* This is a death to self that we do not often consider, yet it was at the heart of the apostle's writings. Through Christ, our closeness to God *begins* where our efforts to reach God *end*. It is at this point that we meet the resurrected Lord and can stand together with Him.

Our escape from the letter of the Law is not to a world where there is no longer right or wrong. Dying to the Law is escaping our independence from God so that we might know union with Christ. Therefore, the proper framework for understanding this difficult concept is relational and not within the finite context of right and wrong or morality.

Discarding the old wages of sin, the new creation lives in the gift of God. Once we have escaped our own good through the cross, *our good becomes the product of our union* with Christ. The Lord never intended for us to be like Him by ourselves; being godly is something the Lord wanted us to do together with Him. Living in separateness is what invited the Lord's wrath, as independence is the foundation and source of all sin. Perhaps that is why we are such miserable failures at being Christ-like when we set out on our own. We either end up with guilt and shame or with pride—it is impossible to be godly without God. Humanity's greatest problem is not behavioral, it is relational. *Our greatest need is God.* For those with the ears to hear it, this is was what the Law was saying.

When we see that death to the Law leads to God, it becomes ridiculous to think dying to the Law leads to more sinfulness. Is the product of union with Christ sin? As Paul might say, "May it never be!" The fruit of our marriage to Christ is love, and love fulfills the Law in every way. However, the letter of the Law tended to lead away from love. The old covenant said love God and God will love you; it also said love God *or else.* Such a system produced fear rather than love, but under the new covenant, God loves first and He loves without condition. Where God is a gift, there is infinite freedom to love God the way He loves us.

The letter of the Law was equally powerless when it came to making people love one another. A world where God was earned was a world filled with condemnation. It was a world of "us and them" rather than a world where everyone is a neighbor.

One of the great contexts of Paul's writings was this transition from being under the Law to be being under grace. If we take the apostle out of this setting, his message can become very confusing, making us believe Paul, the champion of grace, was merely another lawgiver with yet another ministry of condemnation and fear.

In Paul's work, he faced many challenges. The old way of relating to God and each other was still battling the mind of Christ, and there was no place where this struggle was more evident than in the relations between the Jews and the Gentiles. Grace was bringing together, but the old order was still trying to tear apart. This tumultuous blending of Jew and Gentile is another great setting of Paul's letters to his churches because it was a problem everywhere he went. The only solution was the triumph of Christ, and understanding this conflict is vital to understanding Paul.

For in Christ Jesus neither circumcision nor uncircumcision avails anything, but a new creation. (GALATIANS 6:15)

When Paul was alive, staunch, Torah-keeping Jews were coming to Christ alongside lawless, Gentile pagans, though their relations were far from amicable. The things churches divide over today are trivial in comparison, and Paul faced the daunting task of holding the young church together while Jew–Gentile disagreements threatened to tear it apart.

There were followers of Christ who still kept Torah, practicing Sabbath keeping and circumcision among other ordinances. Many defined Christianity as a branch of Judaism, and they saw no need to set aside Moses for Christ. They believed the two could live very well together and even thought it was necessary. To them, the Gentiles had to get circumcised if they desired to follow Christ. If former pagans really wanted to be in good with God, they had to become more like Jews.

Before we condemn the Jewish believers, however, we should acknowledge that the Gentile believers had the same attitude toward the Jews. The Jews thought they were better because they were circumcised, but the Gentiles thought they were better because they were not. From the Gentile viewpoint, they were the ones who were truly living in grace. In Romans, chapters 9 through 11, we learn that some Gentiles believed that God had cut off the Jews completely. He was going with "plan B," and the Gentiles were His new favorites.

But Paul sternly corrected both groups. While the Jews said, "God loves us more" and the Gentiles countered, "No, God loves us more!" Paul was the parent trying to sort out the conflict between siblings. "You are *both* wrong!" he ministered, for being circumcised or not being circumcised had little to do with bringing a person closer to God. What made both Jew and Gentile acceptable to God was Christ, and the same thing—Christ's loving gift—was the bond that would make them acceptable to each other.

We might get the idea that Paul wanted the Jews to become like the Gentiles and leave Torah behind, but there is no evidence he tried to make them do so. If the Jews wanted to keep their culture and traditions, that was fine with Paul. In fact, while among the Jews, Paul himself acted very Jewish.[2] He did, however, want the Jews to understand that Torah keeping was not their righteousness but rather a means of participating in Christ. The Torah's customs and rituals pointed to Christ, but they themselves did not make the Jews righteous.

In contrast to this leniency, the apostle fought fiercely to keep the Gentiles from taking on the rituals of the Jews—though not because such customs were evil. Certain Jews were still presenting Torah as a means to righteousness, a useless persuasion that, in Paul's eyes, was trying to pull the Gentiles back into the old covenant and away from the gift.

It is human nature to think someone has to be like us to be our brother. Likewise, we often believe someone has to be like us to be close to God. But this is the mindset Jesus came to destroy. In the same fashion, Paul wanted both Jew and Gentile to understand that common behavior did not make them one; Christ did, and Christ alone. If the Jews and Gentiles could see this, they could see the glory of the kingdom of God—witness what the letter of the Law had separated and grace had put together—and see the brotherhood between them.

The letter of the Law condemns and makes us condemning; grace compels forgiveness and acceptance. Jesus had an encounter with a woman caught in sin that illustrates this point.

> *Now early in the morning He came again into the temple, and all the people came to Him; and He sat down and taught them. Then the scribes and Pharisees brought to Him a woman caught in adultery. And when they had set her in the midst, they said to Him, "Teacher, this woman was caught in adultery, in the very act. Now Moses, in the law, commanded us that such should be stoned. But what do You say?" This they said, testing Him, that they might have something of which to accuse Him. But Jesus stooped down and wrote on the ground with His finger, as though He did not hear.*

*So when they continued asking Him, He raised Himself up
and said to them, "He who is without sin among you, let him
throw a stone at her first." And again, He stooped down and
wrote on the ground. Then those who heard it, being convicted
by their conscience, went out one by one, beginning with the
oldest even to the last. And Jesus was left alone, and the woman
standing in the midst. When Jesus had raised Himself up and
saw no one but the woman, He said to her, "Woman, where
are those accusers of yours? Has no one condemned you?"*

She said, "No one, Lord."

*And Jesus said to her, "Neither do I condemn you; go and sin
no more."* (JOHN 8:2–11)

Have you ever had rocks thrown at you? I am not talking about
literal stones but words. Words cannot take away our lives, but they
can take away our worth. We human beings are capable of hurling
judgments at each other with deadly accuracy, and we have all been
a target. Maybe someone in your family has taken aim at you and left
you with scars that do not go away. Or perhaps a person or a group of
people has labeled you a transgressor unworthy of their presence.

If so, Jesus came to give back to you what the cruelty of others
took away. He came to speak to your heart and say that, though others
have condemned you, He does not. Others may have withdrawn
from you, but He draws near. He picks you out of a crowd and says,
"You are forgiven." And as He speaks, all the hateful words fade away,
leaving the two of you standing alone. "Where are your accusers?"
He asks. His gift has silenced their voices.

The Lord came for the targets just as much as He came to take the
rocks out of the rock throwers' hands. We have all been one of those,
too. While the Pharisees were right—the Law of Moses demanded
this woman's death—Jesus skillfully made them see that the Law also
condemned them. And what was the Lord writing on the ground?
Some believe He was spelling out the sins of the accusers. Torah
demanded the death of those who broke the Sabbath, and perhaps
Jesus wrote at the feet of some, "Sabbath breaker." This, along with

His words—"He who is without sin among you, let him throw a stone at her first"—would have been stunning. Every man there would have had to face the fact that he deserved to die as much as this woman.

Sometimes we do not know what we are doing when we hurl judgment and condemnation at others. Would we throw a rock at Jesus? The scriptures reveal that this is what we do when we insult our brother. And every rock we have ever thrown may have been carefully aimed at someone we disliked, but Christ felt every blow.

Paul was once the greatest rock thrower of all, and he persecuted God's people. Yet when he encountered the risen Lord on the road to Damascus, Christ said, "Saul, Saul, why are you persecuting Me ?"[3] Then God took the rocks from Saul's hands, and he became Paul, the great hero of grace. Grace can do what the letter of the Law cannot do. It can even turn rock throwers into healers.

The Lord ended His conversation with the woman by saying, "Go and sin no more;" first came grace, and then came change. The Law demands that change comes first, a requirement we are not able to keep. Therefore, as Paul taught, we must die to the Law so that we can be joined to Christ. We die to the law, not so that we can sin all we want but *so that we can have God*. When the woman walked away, she did not leave with a rule to keep; she left with the knowledge that God did not condemn her. He was with her, though others rejected her. God's love freed her to sin no more.

11

Know Your Mountain

For you have not come to the mountain that may be touched and that burned with fire, and to blackness and darkness and tempest, and the sound of a trumpet and the voice of words, so that those who heard it begged that the word should not be spoken to them anymore. For they could not endure what was commanded: "And if so much as a beast touches the mountain, it shall be stoned or shot with an arrow." And so terrifying was the sight that Moses said, "I am exceedingly afraid and trembling."

But you have come to Mount Zion and to the city of the living God, the heavenly Jerusalem; to an innumerable company of angels; to the general assembly and church of the firstborn who are registered in heaven; to God, the Judge of all; to the spirits of just men made perfect; to Jesus, the Mediator of the new covenant; and to the blood of sprinkling that speaks better things than that of Abel. (HEBREWS 12:18–24)

At Mount Sinai, in the time of Moses, God manifested Himself to His people, descending with lightning, thunder, and fire. Smoke, darkness, and blackness shrouded God, so the people could not see

Him, and as He came down, a trumpet began to sound louder and louder until it reached a terrifying pitch. There were no long lines of worshippers eager to climb up the mountain to get closer to the Lord. The people wanted to send Moses to speak for them, but even their great leader trembled in fear.

Not a very inviting picture of God, is it? The ancient Hebrews obviously viewed the Lord much differently than most Christians do today. Who among us would associate darkness and intense fear with God's presence? Imagine a congregation today standing outside a church building, not wanting to go in because God might be in there. "Let's send the pastor. We do not want to go!"

Such a scenario sounds ridiculous to us. We are far more apt to think of God's presence as a peaceful, desirable place rather than a place where we might die. Why is our view of God so different? Some have suggested that people got tired of the unapproachable, angry, scary God of the Old Testament, so they got rid of Him and replaced Him with a loving, approachable God.

Something did change between the Old and New Testaments, but it was not God. It was covenants. The basis of relationship with God changed from Law to grace; boldness replaced fear, and joy pushed out dread. Near to God became the most desirable place to be rather than the last place anyone would want to go.

Covenantal change is one of the most important contexts of the New Testament, yet most people ignore it. Doing so can lead to great confusion in our relationship with God, however. Is He the scary God who does not want us around, or is He the Lord who is more present and intimate than we could ever imagine? Many end up with a mixture of Law and grace, of the old and the new covenants, and it is no wonder we sometimes have trouble relating to the Lord.

To make matters even more confusing, we still hear preaching and teaching that comes straight from Mount Sinai. Fear is its prime motivator and the commandments its sword. Like the ancient Hebrews, we want the God of Sinai's blessing, but we are not sure we want Him or that He wants us. Understanding the new covenant removes all fear. It opens our eyes to see that God is near and His kindness is certain.

The book of Hebrews exhorted the early Christians to choose their mountain and live there. Their choice was either the Law of Sinai or the grace of Zion; there was no living with one foot on one mountain and one foot on the other. The writer of Hebrews spoke of backsliding, only he defined it differently than we do today. To him, backsliding was going back into the old covenant, and obedience was making the journey from the old covenant to the new. It was coming into the glory of who Jesus is and what He has done, and then dwelling there.

In the Old Testament books of Leviticus, Numbers, and Deuteronomy, we see God's requirements of the old covenant people of God. These books contain rules and ordinances concerning everything from morality to temple worship; these are the books of the Law.

The book of Deuteronomy takes the form of an ancient legal contract or treaty.[1] In it, we see what God expected of His people and what God's people could expect of God. It all begins with a condition:

Now it shall come to pass, if you diligently obey the voice of the Lord your God, to observe carefully all His commandments which I command you today, that the Lord your God will set you high above all nations of the earth. (DEUTERONOMY 28:1)

God required that His people be a people of Torah. It was not only to govern their morals but also to set before them a life rich in religious ritual. The Law defined right and wrong, Sabbath keeping, circumcision, feast keeping, sacrifices, and cleanliness laws—Torah keeping was a full-time occupation! It was to permeate the Jews' entire lives, much like a marriage covenant. It is no accident that Yahweh looked at Israel as His wife and that He required she be faithful to Him alone. Torah revealed how the two were to live together. And if the people of God fulfilled the requirement of the Law, God would fulfill His part of the agreement. He would bless them with a life so good they would hardly contain its bounty.

And all these blessings shall come upon you and overtake you, because you obey the voice of the Lord your God:

Blessed shall you be in the city, and blessed shall you be in the country.

Blessed shall be the fruit of your body, the produce of your ground and the increase of your herds, the increase of your cattle and the offspring of your flocks.

Blessed shall be your basket and your kneading bowl.

Blessed shall you be when you come in, and blessed shall you be when you go out.

The Lord will cause your enemies who rise against you to be defeated before your face; they shall come out against you one way and flee before you seven ways.

The Lord will command the blessing on you in your storehouses and in all to which you set your hand, and He will bless you in the land which the Lord your God is giving you.
(DEUTERONOMY 28:2–8)

The Lord promised that if His beloved kept Torah, He would give them a very good life in a very good land. Materially, they would be blessed beyond compare. The early Hebrews spent 400 years in slavery and then forty years wandering in the wilderness. God's promise of a home was no doubt exceptionally sweet.

If the Lord's agreement with Israel included only blessings, there would be little room for concern, but there were also the curses.

But it shall come to pass, if you do not obey the voice of the Lord your God, to observe carefully all His commandments and His statutes which I command you today, that all these curses will come upon you and overtake you:

Cursed shall you be in the city, and cursed shall you be in the country.

Cursed shall be your basket and your kneading bowl.

Cursed shall be the fruit of your body and the produce of your land, the increase of your cattle and the offspring of your flocks.

Cursed shall you be when you come in, and cursed shall you be when you go out...

And it shall be, that just as the Lord rejoiced over you to do you good and multiply you, so the Lord will rejoice over you to destroy you and bring you to nothing; and you shall be plucked from off the land [that] you go to possess.
(DEUTERONOMY 28:15–19, 63)

Actually, if we read all of Deuteronomy 28, we will see that the number of curses in this passage is far greater than the number of blessings. Losing the land of promise was the end and culmination of all the miseries that would come upon God's people if they disobeyed.

Blessings and curses were God's primary motivators in the old covenant relationship. God's favor or disfavor hinged on the faithfulness of His people, and such was nature of Mount Sinai.

We still hear the voice of Sinai in today's church, and its primary motivators are still material blessing and the threat of losing it. Good things will happen to those who do the do's and do not do the don'ts, and bad things will come upon those who fail to measure up. Of course, the do's and don'ts vary from congregation to congregation, but the system is the same. Anything that has our faithfulness at its core is a descendant of the old covenant relationship with God—a relationship that had its glory but ultimately failed.

When God's people entered a covenant with Him based upon their obedience, they did not know where they were going. No doubt, they thought they were headed to a land of delights, believing they could accomplish what God desired and become a people worthy of Yahweh. Little did they know, God had other plans. The relationship they entered would not lead them to a perfection of their own making but to Christ.

The New Testament book of Hebrews is a book about covenants. Its imagery is foreign to us in our day, but when we put it in its covenantal context, it reveals its mysteries.

Hebrews first speaks of the superiority of Christ and how His house has a glory that surpasses that of Moses's. In chapters 3 and 4, we see wilderness imagery as the writer refers back to the ancient Hebrews' wilderness journey to the Promised Land. He says that, through Christ, another exodus was taking place in the first century—one of the spirit and not of the body. *It was a journey of the heart.* God's people were not going from one place on a map to another; they were going from the old covenant to the new.

At the heart of the old covenant promise was the land, and the new covenant promise was a Person. While it is true there was a glory to the faithfulness of God's chosen—when they obeyed, life was good—it could not compare to the glory of the faithfulness of Christ. For Christ came not to restore the good life of the old covenant but to give us Himself. *He* is the abundant life of the new covenant.

The New Testament dwelling is the presence of God, and its greatest blessing is knowing the Lord. In this new home, the glory of the infinite overshadows the glory of the finite; material blessing is secondary. And though the new covenant hinges upon the faithfulness of Christ, His faithfulness is infinite and unwavering. Those making the first century exodus were required to leave behind one glory, but that small glory faded in the greater light of Christ. With the new covenant, Christ brought His people to a place Moses never could: He brought them into the Holiest of Holies and the glory of God.

Blessing comes before obedience and having before doing in the new covenant; our behavior flows from grace. We see this reflected in Christ's ministry, His blessing always coming before His commands, which was astonishing to the Jews of that day. They said, "Surely, we need to get our house in order before the Messiah will come in and bless us!" Yet Jesus went to the messiest places and poured out blessing upon blessing. Anything He required of His followers always followed grace, the exact opposite of the old order, where God gave Himself to His people if they gave themselves to Him. With Christ, God gives Himself without condition, and it is this gift that compels us to give ourselves in return. Love rules in the new Promised Land, not fear or lust. Now love is our primary motivator.

The journey from the old covenant to the new was not without conflict, as Paul learned frequently in his struggle to referee the Jews and Gentiles in the church's early days. In the first century, the old covenant world still existed alongside the new, and those of the righteousness of man persecuted those of the righteousness of Christ. Because the covenantal journey was perilous and costly, the temptation to go back to Mount Sinai was constant. It appeared safe, but returning there would have been like the ancient Hebrews turning away from the Promised Land for Egypt. From a distance, Egypt looked like a safe place to live, but they knew it was bondage. The book of Hebrews uses Exodus imagery to exhort the first-century Jews to resist the old covenant and hold fast to the Lord instead.

Today, we speak very little of covenants because the idea is foreign to us. The old covenant does not overshadow our lives like it did the Jews of the first century, and few of us ever consider things like circumcision, Sabbath keeping, and Old Testament purity rituals. No one offers up sacrifices in Jerusalem to gain God's favor anymore—in many respects the old covenant world is gone. Yet our journey is still similar to our first-century brethren's.

Some might look at our walk with God as if we were still on Sinai, where the goal is to become a better person so we can have a better blessing. If this is our purpose, we are living on the wrong mountain—one that God tore down long ago. Our actual dwelling is Zion, and Zion has a different nature entirely. Here, we walk with God by losing our own righteousness to dwell in the righteousness of Christ. At Sinai, they lived by commands; at Zion, we live in the gift. Here, nourishment and growth come not by an ever-increasing effort to gain God but by God's ever-increasing grace.

It is important to understand that Zion has a different blessing than Sinai. When we walk with God, we may still look for material blessings, expecting the Lord to give us health, prosperity, and a successful life as reward for our devotion. But if this is all we see, we have not yet *seen* Zion. Remember: the great blessing of the new covenant is not finite but infinite, and it is not a thing or a place but

131

a Person. It is God Himself. Yes, there are material blessings at Zion, but they can never replace the ultimate in God.

If we do not understand our mountain, we will have trouble relating to the Lord. We will make promises to start doing this or to stop doing that, then wonder why God does not help us. If material blessings are absent from our lives, we will feel like God has forsaken us. If our troubles are many, we will wonder what we have done wrong. At Sinai, God remains surrounded by a veil of darkness.

Fortunately, the view from Zion is infinitely glorious. From here, we see that God is always giving us the gift, even when He takes something away. God takes so He can give Himself to us—takes away our boast in ourselves, sometimes painfully, that He might replace it with Christ. At Zion, loss leads to gain and every wilderness leads to the new covenant Promised Land. Zion overflows with the light of Christ.

— *12* —

Our Wilderness Journey: Conquered by Love

I have suffered the loss of all things, and count them as rubbish,
that I may gain Christ.... (PHILIPPIANS 3:8)

The way we gain in the kingdom of God confounds the world's wisdom; sometimes the path to the Promised Land goes through a wilderness. Human logic says there is no victory in losing, no glory in weakness, and no gain in loss. Yet it is in the wilderness that such things become our companions and teachers, leading us higher than we can imagine.

The wilderness is not pleasant and can be a confusing place. It is where we ask our most heartfelt, even tortured questions: "Why did this happen to me?" "Why did God take away something/someone I love so dearly?" "Why won't He take away what I do not want in my life?" "Why won't He give me what I need?"

Too often, we chalk up such questions as unanswerable, or we say that all things are working for good, though we are not sure how. Jesus said we are His friends, however, and friends do not get left in the dark. They get to know what their Lord is doing.[1]

As you read this chapter, I pray that God will take you up on a "high mountain" and give you *His view* of the wilderness. May He let

133

you see that the times you thought you were going nowhere, your destination was *certain*. May you see that even when it looked like God was against you, He was *for you*. When it seemed like God was silent, He was *speaking*, and when it appeared God was taking away, He was *giving*. Your greatest failures, your greatest successes, your greatest weaknesses, your greatest strengths—*everything* comes from God as part of your journey into the fullness of the gift.

The wilderness is the place we suffer loss so that we might gain Christ, and I have been to such a place. I still remember the day my church ordained me for ministry. People from the congregation gathered around me, laid their hands on me, and prayed. Many of them spoke dramatic words about all the wonderful things God was going to do in my life. They had high expectations, and so did I.

I was off to Eureka Springs, Arkansas, to be the pastor of Thorncrown Chapel, and I held in my heart the stories of people who had great faith and saw God move in extraordinary ways. I believed I would be one of the rare individuals who prayed heaven *down*—no one I knew prayed as diligently I did! I would often spend entire days in prayer, seeking God's blessing, and countless hours getting my sermons just right.

At first, everything went as planned. Eureka Springs quickly became a premier destination for churches and tour groups, and we had more people coming to the chapel than we could handle. There were times the people waiting to get into Thorncrown lined the entire trail that led from the chapel down to our parking lot, and it wasn't uncommon to have fifty or more buses daily. We held services from the time we opened the chapel doors until the time we closed them.

On Sundays, our first service started at 7:30 AM and was followed by two more services at 9 and 11 AM. And all three were always full, even the early one. Other pastors envied what I had, and people were always telling me what a wonderful job I was doing. It seemed I was well on my way to being great in the kingdom of God.

As I noted earlier, however, walking with God is often a journey that stumps the mind. Sometimes when we think we are fighting for God, we are really fighting against Him. From our perspective, we seem to be walking close to Him, but in reality, we are walking away. Fortunately, God is always there to give a course correction, even when it's a painful one.

At times, God's presence is undeniable. One Saturday, I was at my place of prayer, feverishly asking God to bless the next day's services, and He showed up. I could tell He did not want to talk about my sermon, and I also sensed that somehow everything was about to change.

Shortly after that, Eureka Springs' popularity among church and tour groups began to fall, and it fell fast. The days of fifty buses a day and three full Sunday services ended. Within two years, the number of tour groups visiting Thorncrown Chapel dropped by almost 80 percent, and our Sunday services suffered likewise. We had to lay off employees as our donations dwindled, and all our plans for expansion ceased. One Sunday, I walked in the chapel, ready to preach, and my heart sank when I saw only one person had showed up for church.

People tend to gauge a minister's success by the size of his or her congregation. When someone learns I am a pastor, they almost always ask how big my membership is. But what they really want to know is how important I am, and I began to loathe the question I once loved. Somehow, on the way to becoming "a somebody" in the ministry, I became "a nobody," and I could not understand why.

God had given me the opposite of what He promised, but that is what the wilderness is. It is a place where we seem to have the opposite of what we think God wants us to have. The ancient Hebrews entered such a place; God promised them a land flowing with milk and honey—a land where there would be no lacking. Yet He sent them into a wilderness where there wasn't even enough food or water to survive.

We think it strange that God would do such a thing. Why would God send His servants to a barren place in order to fulfill His promises? God said that Moses would be a deliverer, but before Moses met God at the burning bush, he spent many years in exile herding sheep. We might imagine Moses out in the midst of his herd saying, "Deliverer? I didn't realize God meant sheep!"

In another instance, God made a promise to Joseph that he would rule over his brothers, and the young man ended up in an Egyptian prison. Prison is about as far from ruling as a person can get! Likewise, the Lord said David would be king. Yet before he ever occupied his kingly palace, David made is bed in caves while hiding from Saul.[2]

Indeed, these barren places are a test of our faith, but they also serve a far greater purpose: the wilderness is where we learn *true* humility. And it is the humble that possess the kingdom of God.[3]

> *At that time the disciples came to Jesus, saying, "Who then is greatest in the kingdom of heaven?"*
>
> *Then Jesus called a little child to Him, set him in the midst of them, and said, "Assuredly, I say to you, unless you are converted and become as little children, you will by no means enter the kingdom of heaven. Therefore whoever humbles himself as this little child is the greatest in the kingdom of heaven. Whoever receives one little child like this in My name receives Me."* (MATTHEW 18:1–5)

Despite Jesus's many teachings and gatherings among "the least" of society, the Gospels tell us that the disciples still argued about who would be "the greatest" in Christ's kingdom. Among the twelve, Peter, James, and John might have thought they could claim the title, as these three were closest to Jesus. They got to see and do things that the others did not.

And what were the grounds for these claims? Peter was probably the oldest disciple, and in that day, being the oldest meant a special status much higher than what our modern culture recognizes.[4] This is one reason Peter was bolder and more outspoken than the others; he tried to do things the eldest was expected to do. Peter walked on water (at least for a little while), and he was the one who boldly proclaimed that Jesus was the Messiah at Caesarea Philippi. All these things could have made this disciple think *he* was the greatest of all.

Next, James might have said, "Not so fast! Jesus invited me to see him raise Jarius's daughter from the dead. I got to behold the transfiguration. Maybe *I* am the greatest."

But then John could have argued that he was the most beloved disciple—the one who was always closest to Jesus's side. He could claim the title "the greatest" as well.

Finally, the disciples decided to let Jesus settle the matter. Approaching Him, they asked, "Lord, who will be your right-hand man in the kingdom?" And per usual, Jesus's response probably stunned them: Jesus took a little child, sat him on His lap and said, "You must humble yourself like this little child to be great in my kingdom!"

In Jesus's time, a child had no social status or greatness because he had not earned any importance in society. And he certainly did not have the status that came with age. A young child's only measure of importance was based on who his father was; if his dad was important, he was important, too.

If you think about it, little kids still get their status from their parents. Have you ever heard a child say, "My dad can beat up your dad"? By talking about his father's status, he is talking about his own; his worth is inseparable from his parent's worth. And just as a child is humble because he looks to someone other than himself to find his worth, Christian humility requires us to look to our Father in heaven to find our value.

Jesus ended His discourse by saying, "Whoever receives one little child like this in My name receives Me." In other words, when the disciples—*anyone*—could see that this small child had no less worth than Caesar himself, they could see the kingdom of God. Only then could they embrace their own importance.

It may sound simple, but it often takes a grueling trek through the wilderness for us grownups to find such faith. When the crowds disappeared from Thorncrown Chapel, I thought God had forsaken me. In reality, He was rescuing me. If I had continued to measure my worth by the greatness of my ministry, I would not have found Christ as the measure of my worth. If the Lord had let my efforts succeed, I never would have rested in the deeds of Christ. *I had to become like a child who had nothing but his Father's love to see clearly.*

If I had never gotten lost in the wilderness, I never would have known the way home—or even what home was. Christ is my dwelling, and the freedom He gives is different than we imagine. I believed freedom was getting a large ministry, so the Lord led me to a place where I did not need a great ministry to *be* great. That is true freedom. Seeking our worth in anything but Christ puts us on a road that leads away from God no matter how good our intentions are. It is a road that is forever lacking.

I believed how much I prayed, how many things I did for God, or how many people came to church on Sunday were the measures of how much God was in my life, and the Lord broke my attachment to such things so I could see that His presence is a gift. He took away the adoring crowds to take away my own righteousness. Without God's mercy, God's presence would have always been a place I was getting to but never arriving in. I once thought a little better sermon and a little more prayer would make heaven come down; I learned in the wilderness that heaven came down a long time ago in the Person of Jesus Christ.

Even when God is taking away, He is giving. If the Lord leads us into a wilderness, He will meet us there and give Himself to us, and we will have more than enough. The wilderness is the place where we come face to face with trials we cannot bear and weaknesses we cannot overcome, but even these lead to Christ.

And lest I should be exalted above measure by the abundance of the revelations, a thorn in the flesh was given to me, a messenger of Satan to buffet me, lest I be exalted above measure. Concerning this thing I pleaded with the Lord three times that it might depart from me. And He said to me, "My grace is sufficient for you, for My strength is made perfect in weakness." Therefore most gladly I will rather boast in my infirmities, that the power of Christ may rest upon me. Therefore I take pleasure in infirmities, in reproaches, in needs, in persecutions, in distresses, for Christ's sake. For when I am weak, then I am strong. (2 CORINTHIANS 12:7–10)

As mentioned in chapter 1, there is much debate over Paul's mysterious thorn in the flesh. Some take the word "flesh" literally, saying the apostle had some sort of illness or physical problem. They suggest an eye ailment, because the one time he actually penned part of one of his epistles with his own hand, he wrote with very large letters.[5] Maybe he could not see well.

However, if we put this passage in its context, it becomes apparent what Paul's thorn in the flesh was. It was trouble—distress followed him constantly! 2 Corinthians, chapter 11, reveals that Paul's enemies beat him with whips and rods numerous times. He was stoned, shipwrecked, and imprisoned. Everywhere he went, someone wanted to kill him.

We might think that Paul faced all these things with unwavering faith and courage, never losing his peace, but that is not so. In his own words, Paul said his troubles were at times so great that he "despaired even of life."[6] In asking the Lord to make the pressure stop, the apostle was asking God to give him a life he could bear. Paul did not like being weak, but his weaknesses had very important work to do in his life. God allowed these ailments to remain to help Paul to know and live in grace.

The wilderness is where we learn from our inabilities, yet it is very important that we understand *what* they are trying to teach us. As it was with Paul, a weakness might be an overwhelming trial or an unmet need. It can also be a temptation or addiction that we cannot overcome. And as much as we beg God to remove it, He seems to have no interest in doing so. Grandiose stands of faith, sincere promises to repent, even fits of anger—all fail to persuade Him. *Reacting from a place of self*, we try so hard to change, and the Lord holds steady with our troubles, front and center.

People tell us that we need to have more faith or that we need to try harder to overcome our weaknesses, but I think Paul would disagree. Instead, *we need to pay attention* to what our weaknesses are trying to tell us.

Our shortcomings are some of our best teachers, and they should not cause us to hide in shame. Rather, they are here to lead us to grace. If we think our weaknesses are telling us to become someone God can accept, we are missing their point: *by our weaknesses, we possess grace.* Those who have the gift of God's acceptance firmly in their heart *despite* their weaknesses are the true victors. By living in God's love even on our worst day, we truly possess God's love. If we believe God's kindness lessens even one iota when we are weak, we have not come to grips with grace.

Ironically, we cannot change our lives until we realize grace does not depend on our being strong. Only the person who knows she does not have to change to have God *truly* has God—this is the great lesson our weaknesses and shortcomings teach us. God allows them to be our companion in the wilderness to show us just how big grace is.

Inabilities are facilitators of union with Christ, not causes for separation. A victor, or one who overcomes, is not necessarily someone who is strong but someone who is joined with Christ. When we see our union with the Lord is unbreakable, we are strong, but *we cannot learn such lessons through strength.* Only in the midst of our greatest shortcomings can we behold the beauty of God's grace; only here does God's strength become our strength. Therefore, we are not to despise our weaknesses; we are to learn all they have to teach us about God. They, as much as our strengths, are part of our journey into God's gift.

The wilderness is the place where failure turns to victory.

Thorncrown Chapel was my dad's dream. In 1971, my father, Jim Reed, a retired schoolteacher, purchased the land where the chapel now stands and built his retirement home there, planning to spend the rest of his life in the peaceful seclusion of the Ozarks. He wasn't the only one who admired his location, however, and people would often stop near his house to gain a better view of the beautiful Ozark hills. Instead of fencing them out, Dad chose to invite them in. And then he decided he and Mom should build a glass chapel in the woods to inspire their visitors.

At first, his friends and family opposed the idea. We all thought Dad was an unlikely servant of God. He did not go to church, and for most of his life, he showed little interest in spiritual things. Why would he suddenly want to do something for God, and why would God choose Dad to do something for Him? My dad was a very persistent fellow, however, and he kept talking about his idea until we all reluctantly gave him our blessing.

The first major obstacle was finding an architect. Who could design the kind of structure my dad wanted, and who would be willing to take on such a project? Dad found his answer unexpectedly one morning while having an early breakfast with a friend. The two were discussing the problem when a man sitting nearby walked over and tapped him on the shoulder. The man apologized for eavesdropping but explained that he knew E. Fay Jones, an architecture professor at the University of Arkansas at Fayetteville. The fellow assured my dad that there was no better man for the job.[7] Shortly thereafter, Dad met Fay Jones, and much to my dad's surprise, Jones was quick to accept the project.

From the first, it seemed God's hand was in everything, even Thorncrown's location. On March 23, 1979, the construction crew broke ground on the mountainside, where Jones originally planned to build the chapel, and was just a day away from pouring the foundation when God put the brakes on. Dad was taking a look around the site when he felt a strange sensation. Though he was alone, he felt like someone was gently pushing him, as if to say, "Walk this way!" When Dad reached Thorncrown's current site, the urging stopped. He looked around. Before him was what looked like a natural stone altar. To his right stood majestic rock bluffs and to his left was a beautiful wooded setting. There was no question that *this* was the spot, and Jones agreed. It seemed like everything was falling into place.

Halfway through the project, however, funds began to run out. The building process soon ground to a halt, and Dad desperately tried to raise the necessary money to complete his dream. First, he went to several banks to try to get a loan, but none would take a risk on such an unusual idea. Next, he wrote all his friends, thinking someone would surely help him. Few responded, and the ones who did chided him, saying that a retired schoolteacher should not be building a glass chapel.

Finally, Dad stepped out one evening to take what he thought would be one last walk down to his half-finished dream. He told himself that he would allow himself one final look and never return. Questions filled his mind: "Why would God do this to someone who is trying to serve Him?" "Why would the Lord give a person a great idea and then abandon him?"

Then, just as Dad was about to leave his dream behind, he did something he had never done before. On the still incomplete altar, he fell on his knees and he prayed. And though Dad had prayed before, it was never on his knees and never like this. He wept and cried, and in the midst of his travail, he found he was not alone.

There, in that lowly place, Dad had a revelation. Sometimes we set out to serve God, and we believe a divine mission or work for God is our destination. Yet we do not know that our real destination is God Himself. For my father, it was his failure to serve God that ultimately led him to God. The Lord never wanted Dad to build a chapel for Him; He wanted to build a chapel *with* Dad, giving Himself to my father in the process. The two began to walk as one when Dad reached the end of himself.

That evening, Dad grabbed hold of the gift, or maybe *it* grabbed hold of *him*. When he got up from his knees, he knew he had entered the realm of God's possibilities. More importantly, he had a relationship with Christ that would change his life. Three days later, a woman in Illinois loaned him all the money he needed to finish the chapel.

Now I could tell you about all the awards Thorncrown has since won and about how famous it has become, but that is not the point. The real miracle is that, on his knees, my dad went from chapel builder to a man who knew God and possessed the gift of God's presence. He navigated out of the wilderness by the path of his trials and sorrows—a map to the Lord that had been there all along.

Dad's failure and God's grace shaped the destiny of Thorncrown Chapel, but not in the way you might think. Thorncrown's purpose is not to point to what a great man did for God; its story is about what a great God did for a man He loved. It is the plot and potential of *everybody's* story. Today, Thorncrown's elegant beauty continues to speak in harmony with the glory of creation. "God is present," it quietly says. "Come participate in who He is."

The wilderness is a place where we wrestle with God and lose in order to win the ultimate prize.

> *But He gives more grace. Therefore He says: "God resists the proud, but gives grace to the humble."* (JAMES 4:6)

The scriptures tell us that God opposes proud people and He blesses humble people, but we need to understand why this is so.

We human beings dislike arrogant people because prideful people diminish other people's worth to increase their own. No one enjoys being diminished, so people typically don't enjoy arrogant people either.

To further this perspective, we note that God, our shining example, is not prideful. Though He is above us, He has no need to prove it. But some still say that God humbles us to put us in our place. He is God, we are not, and He wants us to know it. That said, we humans also recognize that those who need to prove themselves superior are often insecure in their own worth. And God is not insecure. He has no desire to prove He is better than us. Our place is at His side, not groveling at His feet.

Indeed, God lowers the proud, but He does this so He can raise them up. God resists pride because it stands in the way of the gift; it closes the door on grace and shuts it tight. *The purpose of humility is to receive grace.* In the wilderness, God deals with *our* resistance to His love. And God wrestles with us not to show that He is stronger but to *give Himself* to us.

In the book of Daniel, we read the story of a self-important king who thought he had it all until God stood in his way. Nebuchadnezzar was the ruler of Babylon and the most powerful man on Earth, and God used the arrogant ruler to bring judgment upon Jerusalem.

And bring judgment he did. In 597 BC, Nebuchadnezzar sacked Jerusalem, destroying the Temple and taking many Jews back to Babylon as slaves. (It is from this time period we get the story of Daniel and the lion's den.) Next, Nebuchadnezzar built an enormous, solid-gold idol that was nine feet wide and ninety feet tall. He commanded that all bow and worship his creation, and in a roundabout way, he was demanding that all worship him. (No doubt the idol bore an uncanny resemblance to the king himself.) No one dared oppose the great Nebuchadnezzar—until three brave young Hebrews came along. Shadrach, Meshach, and Abed-Nego refused to bow down before the idol, and the king's response was likewise extreme. Nebuchadnezzar had some pretty impressive ovens he used to smelt all that gold, and he ordered the men to be cast in one of them.

But God still had plans for Nebuchadnezzar. Though Shadrach, Meshach, and Abed-Nego stood in the midst of the fiery oven, they did not burn. In fact, when the king looked inside, he saw *four* men standing in the blaze (perhaps an Old Testament appearance of Christ). Nebuchadnezzar was so affected that he repented and praised the God of the Hebrews.

Unfortunately, the king soon returned to his arrogance. The Lord warned Nebuchadnezzar in a dream that he would soon lose everything if he did not turn from his pride, but the king ignored Him. Finally, the day came when the king's dream turned into his worst nightmare: Nebuchadnezzar not only lost all his material possessions, he also lost his mind. Humanity cast him away, and he lived in the wilderness like an animal for seven years. Then one day, the once prideful king looked up.

And at the end of the time I, Nebuchadnezzar, lifted my eyes to heaven, and my understanding returned to me; and I blessed the Most High and praised and honored Him who lives forever.... (DANIEL 4:34)

In Nebuchadnezzar's words, we see the essence of humility: *he lifted his eyes to heaven.* We do not humble ourselves by pondering how weak or insignificant we are; in fact, we do not ponder ourselves at all. True humility is taking our eyes off of ourselves and looking at Christ. Sometimes we get the idea that the worse we feel about ourselves, the more God likes it. But feeling worthless is still self-focus, and self-focus is false humility.

Humility is not looking down but *up*. It is seeing the glory of who Christ is and letting Him, rather than self, become the measure of who we are and what we have.

Jesus used a bowl of water and a towel to teach His disciples this lesson. When the Lord lowered Himself to wash the disciples' feet, Peter protested. In that day, foot washing was something a servant did for his master, never the other way around. Peter did not think he was worthy to have Jesus wash his feet—a gesture we might consider to be humility. And had that been the case, we'd expect the Lord to praise His disciple: "Yes, you are unworthy, and don't you forget it!" Instead, Jesus gently chastised Peter, saying, "If I do not wash you, you have no part with Me."[8] In other words, if Peter did not let Jesus give him this great gift, he could not have the Lord either. Peter was fighting the *ultimate* gift.

Surprisingly, faith and humility are very closely related, working *together*—not in opposition—to bring us to the gift, as both involve looking away from ourselves and seeing Christ. Yet just as there can be a false humility, there can be a false faith. Sometimes, in the midst of our trials, we think that God's greatest desire is for us to hold on; we believe He is testing our faith. And if our faith is big enough and we hold on to the promise without letting go, God will get us through our troubles. Little do we know that if our eyes are on "our faith," our eyes are still on ourselves. We are robbing God of His glory by trying to be worthy of the gift.

If necessary, our wilderness wanderings will lead us to the end of our ability to hold on to God. When we reach the end of "our faith," we can see what true faith is. It is seeing that *God holds on to us*. Even if we let go, God does not. Humble faith is seeing that Christ's victory has trumped our ability to fail; *He* is the Victor. There are no exceptions.

This is the magnificent vision Nebuchadnezzar saw. And when he did, God restored all his wealth and power *and more*. At long last, he had God. Likewise, when we come to see that *Christ* is King and bow our hearts to Him, we come to know—to truly *have*—grace and love forever.

"Brokenness" is a word that has all but left the consciousness of modern Christianity. When we speak of God's hand being in our lives, we think of Him delivering us from our troubles or giving us what we want. We almost never think of God taking away our dreams or allowing a thorn in our flesh. Yet these things are very much a part of our walk with God. And His actions accomplish more than bending us to His will. A broken person is not one who simply says, "Okay, God. You win. I will do what You want." God's dealings have a much more fundamental purpose: His deepest work with us is not about our doing or not doing but about our *receiving*. In the wilderness, God defeats our opposition to the gift.

To obey God is to receive union with Christ; it is not another promise to do better and finally get our lives together. Such promises only reveal that we have not learned the wilderness's lessons. God wants to give us Himself, and the broken person takes the gift.

Like the Pharisees, we often oppose God without knowing it, thinking we are doing the will of God when we are really fighting Him. The more I earnestly tried to get God to be with me, the faster I was running *away* from Him. By trying to earn God's love, I was degrading it—even trampling upon it. Yet love pursued and overcame me anyway. *There is no more blessed person than the one conquered by love.*

Our time in the wilderness will seem like wandering until we understand why we are there. Our trials—seemingly unanswered prayers and personal failures—will seem pointless. But when we see that the wilderness is the place where our religion becomes a love relationship with God, it becomes a place of beauty. We may never want to leave, thanking God that He led us there. For it is often in the most desolate place that we see the gift, and we see that it is ours.

Seeing

When Jesus came into the region of Caesarea Philippi, He asked His disciples, saying, "Who do men say that I, the Son of Man, am?"

So they said, "Some say John the Baptist, some Elijah, and others Jeremiah or one of the prophets."

He said to them, "But who do you say that I am?"

Simon Peter answered and said, "You are the Christ, the Son of the living God."

Jesus answered and said to him, "Blessed are you, Simon Bar-Jonah, for flesh and blood has not revealed this to you, but My Father who is in heaven. And I also say to you that you are Peter, and on this rock I will build My church, and the gates of Hades shall not prevail against it." (MATTHEW 16:13–18)

The world had never seen a love as big as Christ's, and His words and works challenged people's ideas about God. Some loved Him for it, and some hated Him for it. And here, at Caesarea Philippi, Jesus pushed the boundaries of His disciples' understanding of grace, revealing that His victory would not only encompass Israel but the whole Earth. And it would do so in this life as well as the life to come.

The original King James Version of the Bible translates verse 18 of the above passage to say that "the gates of hell shall not prevail" against Christ's church. However, some of the words the original King James Version translates as "hell" it probably should not. The King James Version is one translation, albeit a good one, but it has its strengths and weaknesses, too.

If we think Jesus was talking about hell in the traditional since, this passage does not make sense. Why would the church want to storm the gates of hell? Is there any place in the Bible that says the church would or should do such a thing? "Hades," the word we see in the original Greek text, fits perfectly, however. Hades is the equivalent of the Old Testament *Sheol*, the place of the dead.

We might think that the Old Testament people of God went to heaven when they died, but according to the scriptures, they did not. Sin separated humanity from God not only in this life but also in the next. The dead were not in heaven but in *Sheol* or Hades, and the tradition of Jesus's day said that Hades had two huge gates. And these gates remained locked, awaiting the day the Messiah would come to set the captives free and take them into God's presence.

At Caesarea Philippi, Jesus was saying that day was upon them. We also see this concept in the book of Revelation, where Jesus, the risen Lord, says "I am He who lives and was dead, and behold, I am alive forevermore. Amen. And I have the keys of Hades and of Death."[1]

The early church understood this concept of separation from God well. An ancient sermon from a fellow named Melito (AD 195) describes Christ and this thought in a most profound way.

> *But He rose from the dead*
> *and mounted up to the heights of heaven.*
> *When the Lord had clothed Himself with humanity,*
> *and had suffered for the sake of the sufferer,*
> *and had been bound for the sake of the imprisoned,*
> *and had been judged for the sake of the condemned,*
> *and buried for the sake of the one who was buried,*

He rose up from the dead
and cried with a loud voice:
Who is he that contends with me?
Let him stand in opposition to me.
I set the condemned man free;
I give the dead man life;
I raised up one who had been entombed.
Who is my opponent?
I, He says, am the Christ.
I am the one who destroyed death,
and triumphed over the enemy,
and trampled Hades underfoot,
and bound the strong one,
and carried off man
to the heights of heaven.
I, He says, am the Christ.[2]

Melito paints a bold picture of Christ, the Victor. Yet if we look closely at Jesus's statement in Matthew 16, we will see that the Lord's victory is for *this* life, not just the afterlife.

Jesus's proclamation took place at Caesarea Philippi, which was no accident. If you recall the first-century history discussed in chapter 5, Herod the Great's son Philip changed the name of this city from Paneas to Caesarea Philippi in honor of Caesar and himself. Caesarea Philippi was one of the most pagan places in all of Palestine,[3] and most devout Jews avoided it altogether. But Jesus went there deliberately.

On a bluff in a rocky part of the city were two temples: one to honor Caesar and another built for the Greek god Pan—both of which the Jews considered blasphemous. The latter, in fact, was the worldwide center for Pan worship, where the followers of Pan demonstrated their devotion by performing acts too lewd to mention. And true to the "wickedness," right next to Pan's temple was a great crevice or crack in the ground said to be the place where dead spirits went to and from Hades. It was called "The Gates of Hell" by the translators of the King James Version, though its actual name was "The Gates of Hades."

By choosing such a controversial location to proclaim that the Gates of Hades would not prevail against His church, Jesus was saying His victory would not only encompass the afterlife but this life as well. Neither Caesar nor paganism would prevail against His people, and history shows us that His words came true. Though Rome and paganism tried to snuff out the light of the Gospel, they were not able to do so.

The Lord's words had an even more powerful meaning, however. Jesus strategically took His disciples to the most sinful, Caesar-glorying place in Palestine to give the revelation of who He was. And it is here that our ideas about God might be challenged a bit. Some people say God only visits holy places—that He only dwells in places where He feels welcome. Where there is sin, God vacates the premises. (Many teach that God is offended quite easily. This is more of an old covenant concept of God, which people have tried to drag over in the new covenant age.) If this were true, what was the Lord of Lords doing in Caesarea Philippi? Why did He make it a point to go to the most sinful places to seek fellowship with the most sinful people?

We sometimes embrace the idea that there are places where God is not present, fragmenting our lives into instances when God is with us and instances when He is not. If our lives were a house, we'd assign some rooms where Christ is present—rooms where we collect the times when we do the right thing—because we believe He is present in our strengths. It only makes sense that Christ wants to be with us when we pray, study the Bible, and go to church, right? He draws near when we do good things.

However, in our house there are also the dark rooms—places Jesus does not want to go and places we do not want Him to visit. These rooms are filled with weakness and failure. Not only do we not want the Lord to see these places, we do not want other people to see them either.

When it comes to our lives, we can have a revival mentality: clean up the hidden rooms, make them comfortable for God, and He will fill the whole house. There is a glory in such thinking, but like the glory that shone from the face of Moses, it is fading.[4] Revivals are always short-lived. The house gets dirty, we do not pray or repent enough, our zeal fades, and God leaves the building—or at least we *think* He does.

Remember: new covenant victory does not begin with doing but with *seeing*. God's presence is a gift. Therefore, God's nearness is *something we perceive*, not something we achieve. We overcome when we see that Jesus is in the darkest room in the house, too. The whole house belongs to Him.

Grace is God being where we think He should not be. We see this profoundly in Jesus's visit to Caesarea Philippi and in His entire ministry. If a person wanted to find Jesus, he could go to the worst sinners and most unclean people, and the Lord would be there. Likewise, we should look for Jesus in the midst of our greatest weaknesses because that is where He wants to be.

The victors are those who see the gift and live in it; they are not those who have the neatest house and the fewest dark rooms. The first step to overcoming is not trying to clean up the darkest room in the house. Rather, it is seeing that the Lord is just as present there as He is in the brightest room in the house. It is God's love that turns darkness into light.

The Apostle Paul would agree that *seeing is vital* in experiencing the victory of Christ, not only in our own lives but in the whole world. Consider his prayer for the church at Ephesus.

> *Therefore I also, after I heard of your faith in the Lord Jesus and your love for all the saints, do not cease to give thanks for you, making mention of you in my prayers: that the God of our Lord Jesus Christ, the Father of glory, may give to you the spirit of wisdom and revelation in the knowledge of Him, the eyes of your understanding being enlightened; that you may know what is the hope of His calling, what are the riches of the glory of His inheritance in the saints, and what is the exceeding greatness of His power toward us who believe, according to the working of His mighty power which He worked in Christ when He raised Him from the dead and seated Him at His right hand in the heavenly places, far above all principality and power and might and dominion, and every name that is named, not only in this age but also in that which is to come.*

And He put all things under His feet, and gave Him to be head over all things to the church, which is His body, the fullness of Him who fills all in all. (EPHESIANS 1:15–23)

Ephesus was a tough place to be a Christian. It was the largest city in Asia Minor and the worldwide center for Diana worship. (She was the Greek nature and fertility goddess.) The local legends said that a statue of Diana fell from the sky, so, of course, they built a temple where it landed.

Diana's temple took 220 years to build and was one of the wonders of the ancient world. In that day, the building was the largest in existence, measuring 220 feet by 425 feet. One hundred and twenty-seven columns, each 60 feet high, supported it, and the entire structure was made of pure white marble. Sitting on a hill overlooking the city, the temple shone down gloriously, as if to say, "Diana is in charge here."[5]

There was also a very powerful contingent of Judaizers in Ephesus (the fellows who wanted to kill Paul). In 1 Corinthians, Paul wrote that he wrestled with wild beasts at this city, and scholars agree that he was not talking about literal animals; he was describing the ferocity of his opponents. It was in Asia that Paul "despaired even of life."[6] Yet from the midst of his lowliness came Paul's great revelation of the triumph of Christ in what we know as the book of Ephesians.

Diana wasn't the only ruler in town, however. Overshadowing the goddess and the Judiazers was the power of Rome, and the Romans portrayed Caesar as a god. People had to bow to him or face the wrath of the mightiest empire the Earth had ever known. Rome portrayed Caesar as the savior of the world.

In 9 BC, the Romans issued the following proclamation about Caesar Augustus, who was the ruler of Rome at the time of Christ's birth:

Since the providence that has divinely ordered our existence has applied her energy and zeal, and has brought to life the most perfect good in Augustus, whom she filled with virtues for the benefit of mankind, bestowing him upon us and our decedents as savior. He who put an end to war and will order peace, Caesar, who by his epiphany exceeded the hopes of those who prophesied good tidings, not only outdoing benefactors of the past but also allowing no hope of greater benefactions in the future.[7]

Later in this passage, the writer calls Augustus a god, so it is easy to see why the early Christians had trouble with Rome. Much of what the early believers said of Christ, Rome also said of Caesar. To make matters worse, when Paul wrote his letter to the Ephesian church, Nero, who was insanely convinced of his own divinity, ruled Rome. The tension between the church and the power that ruled the world was about to escalate.

In the midst of all these authorities and powers, Paul prayed for the church at Ephesus. He could have prayed many things for this seemingly overmatched group of believers, but he prayed only one thing: *what they needed most was to see.*

Christ was above all who opposed the church, and the church was in Christ. Therefore, the church, too, was above all rule, authority, and power. Paul knew that if his beloved church members could see with their hearts that Jesus's death and resurrection made Him triumph over the whole city of Ephesus, they could overcome as well. Diana could not keep God out of the city no matter how sinful her followers were, nor could Caesar's legions bar the city from God's love. Christ was in charge inside the church walls and everywhere— there was no place He was not Lord. Grace had taken over, and thus the gift reigned supreme.

In defining the world around us today, we face the same choice as the church members in Ephesus long ago: we can look out the window and focus on how bad things are, or we can look at Jesus and the gift. Christ is the measure of how much God is in the church, but He is also the measure of how much God is out there in everyday life, beyond Sunday and Wednesday meetings. Because of Christ, there is no place that is without God, and there is no place that does not belong to Him.

God wants us to live fully in His triumph. To do so, however, *we must see as He does.* And what do we usually see when we look at the world—a place God adores or a place He abhors? The gift defines us as much as it defines *all* of God's creation. In other words, how big is God's gift? Does it know any limit, any boundaries? When Christ rose from the grave, grace took over in every possible way; the infinite came to dwell in the finite. All that remains is for us to open our eyes—and our hearts—to His great victory.

In our day, we write books about the world's dire state, filling their pages with stories of how dark the darkness is. Like our lives, we compartmentalize on a larger scale as well, dividing the world into places where God is and places where He is not. Yet the way to overcome the darkness is not to glorify it; it is to see the light *in spite of* the dark. Our job is to see—and then help others to see—the glory of Christ and what He has done.

How we view the world is a reflection of our own relationship with God. If grace does not reign out there, it cannot reign in us. We can no more keep God's presence out of our lives any more than the worldly powers could keep God out of Ephesus. Christ is the King who rules in grace, and, as such, His reign will *always* be victorious.

If we can see grace in the most sinful places on Earth, there is no place we cannot see it in our own lives. The glory of Christ changes humanity's consciousness; Paul called it a renewed mind.[8] The gift changes what we see when we look in the mirror, and it changes what we see when we look at our neighbor. It even changes what we see when we look in the eyes of our worst enemy.

Looking at Jesus redefines everything. The worst sinner is merely one forsaken of God until we look at Jesus. One glimpse of the Lord, and we no longer see the downtrodden but the beloved—persons whom God is near. Jesus is the light in the darkness. When we see a world whose every inch belongs to Him, we witness a place where grace reigns—a place no longer ugly but clothed in the beauty of God's love.

Today, we face a whole new set of problems, but Paul's prayer for us would still be the same as that for his church in Ephesus. In the midst of all our troubles, what do we need most? We need to see Jesus, for we only see ourselves and our world clearly—*we only see the gift clearly*—when we look at Him.

The Life

We have seen in previous chapters that one of the most important contexts of the New Testament is covenantal transition; God was giving a new definition of righteousness in the time of Christ. In the old covenant, to be righteous, one had to keep Torah. In the new covenant, *Christ* has become our righteousness. Now, when a person thinks of righteousness, he must not think of himself but of Christ.

Likewise, when the new covenant came, God gave a new definition of abundant life. The Old Testament stories tell of the great wealth and status God gave those who obeyed him. From Abraham to the kings of Israel and Judah, a righteous person was a prosperous person. And as it was with Job, even when God took away, He always gave back more than He had taken.[1] In the New Testament, the definition of prosperity changes. Now, a truly blessed life is not merely one filled with finite things but one filled with the infinite Christ. *He* is abundant life.

In the book of Deuteronomy, God gave an extensive list of the blessings He would give to those who kept Torah—among them, prosperity and a secure land in which to dwell.[2] If we read these promises carefully, we will notice that every one of them is material. The Lord guaranteed a good life for all who simply obeyed Him.

When we come to the new covenant, however, we see an amazing shift in emphasis.

Blessed be the God and Father of our Lord Jesus Christ, who has blessed us with every spiritual blessing in the heavenly places in Christ.... (EPHESIANS 1:3)

In the New Testament, the overwhelming focus becomes spiritual blessings, or what Jesus called "treasure in heaven." The old covenant blessings were temporal; the new, eternal. The old promise was a place to dwell; the new is to dwell in Christ. And while the old was a good life, the new is *Christ as our life*. In John, chapter 14, we see Jesus's astonishing proclamation of this: "I am the way, the truth, and the life."[3]

Just as someone in the first century had to change his definition of righteousness from the self to Christ, a new covenant sojourner had to change his definition of "the life" from earthly things to Christ. Just as his journey from the righteousness of man to the righteousness of Christ involved loss, so did his journey to the abundant life Christ promised. And it was a loss many were not willing to suffer.

John, chapter 6, takes place over two days, each of which is a picture of the different covenants. The first day, Jesus offered the people the old covenant blessing; the second day, He offered them the new covenant blessing. Interestingly, they loved Him the first day, but He troubled them the second.

Jesus was at the height of His popularity at the beginning of this chapter. Five thousand people had come to hear Him preach and to watch Him do His works, but somehow, everyone in attendance had forgotten to bring lunch—everyone except one young boy. The lad had five barley loaves and two small fish. (Barley loaves were the food of the poor. They were very small and flat, so a person had to eat many of them to get full.[4]) It wasn't much of a meal, but it was all Jesus needed. The Lord gave thanks, and suddenly, there were more than enough loaves and fishes to feed every one of the 5,000.

A free lunch might be more common in our day, but we live in a day of abundance. Roman taxation in Jesus's day made people poor and hungry. Among the curses God listed in the book of Deuteronomy was Gentile-inflicted oppression along with hunger and thirst. The Jews had all of these troubles and more in the first century, and it would have been easy to believe God had turned against them. A full belly was one of the great blessings of the old covenant. When Jesus fed the multitude, the people began to believe that the Lord might actually be the one who would restore God's favor.

It's no wonder the people misinterpreted Jesus's gesture, getting so excited they thought He was the Savior/King who would bring back the glory of old-covenant Israel. They'd been waiting for a ruler to lead them back to the good life God promised in the Torah—a life of prosperity, free from pagan oppression. Israel would be once again be on top of the world, where it rightfully belonged. On that first day in John, chapter 6, it appeared Jesus might be such a deliverer.

Many have the same mindset in our day, wanting Jesus to be like He was with the loaves and the fishes. We long for a Messiah who will take care of all our problems, give us what we want, and put *us* on top of the world. Some still preach a first-day Jesus: "Come to Jesus, and He will fix your life. He will make you prosperous and happy, ridding you of every trouble." And some people still love the first-day Jesus just as the masses who experienced His works in John, chapter 6. He continues to attract huge crowds and generate a lot of excitement—He is a very popular fellow! One sure way to gather a following is to stay with the Jesus of the first day.

Yet John, chapter 6, does not end with the first day. A second day came and everything changed.

We can imagine the multitude waking up that next morning, eager to find their beloved Messiah. Maybe He would do another miracle! That bread and fish tasted pretty good, and it was nice not to feel hungry at the end of the day.

Jesus seemed to have disappeared, however. After His great miracle, the Lord withdrew to be by Himself, and His disciples headed across the Sea of Galilee to Capernaum. How would the Lord catch up to them without transportation? Being the Son of God, it was not a problem. Jesus simply walked on the water until He got to the disciples' boat! When the crowds finally found Him in Capernaum, they could not imagine how He got there (and the disciples were not telling).

> *Jesus answered them and said, "Most assuredly, I say to you, you seek Me, not because you saw the signs, but because you ate of the loaves and were filled. Do not labor for the food which perishes, but for the food which endures to everlasting life, which the Son of Man will give you, because God the Father has set His seal on Him."*
>
> *Then they said to Him, "What shall we do, that we may work the works of God?"*
>
> *Jesus answered and said to them, "This is the work of God, that you believe in Him whom He sent."*
>
> *Therefore they said to Him, "What sign will You perform then, that we may see it and believe You? What work will You do? Our fathers ate the manna in the desert; as it is written, 'He gave them bread from heaven to eat.'"*
>
> *Then Jesus said to them, "Most assuredly, I say to you, Moses did not give you the bread from heaven, but My Father gives you the true bread from heaven. For the bread of God is He who comes down from heaven and gives life to the world."*
>
> *Then they said to Him, "Lord, give us this bread always."*
>
> *And Jesus said to them, "I am the bread of life. He who comes to Me shall never hunger, and he who believes in Me shall never thirst."* (JOHN 6:26–35)

On the second day, the people wanted more bread; they wanted Jesus to show them how to do the same miracles He did. Instead, He offered them not the bread that fills the stomach but the bread of life, *which fills the soul.* The first-day Jesus gave the people the old covenant blessing—a material gift. But on the second day, He offered them the new covenant blessing—a spiritual, *infinite gift*— embodied in a Person; Jesus offered them Himself. *He* is the second-day blessing, the great promise of the new covenant.

Jesus said He came that we might have life "more abundantly."[5] Many take this to mean that through Christ, God will give us a good life filled with wealth, health, and every good thing. While the new covenant does include material blessings, they are secondary at best. The primary blessing is God Himself, and our relationship with Him makes our lives forever full. But most of the people who loved Jesus that first day turned away from Him the second.

From that time many of His disciples went back and walked with Him no more. (JOHN 6:66)

Eternal life is the great new covenant promise. And when we hear the word "eternal," we often think of a length of time—a no-expiration-date ticket to heaven, reserved for the future date of our mortal death. John's Gospel compels us to equate it with Christ, however. In chapter 17, verse 3, of his Gospel, John provides this definition: "And this is eternal life, that they may know You, the only true God, and Jesus Christ, whom You have sent." *Eternal life is a Person*, and we experience it when we partake of Christ and what He has done for us. The gift of God is for today and forever.

When we share the Gospel with people, we often tell them that if they receive Jesus, they will go to heaven. While true, this is not the heart of the Gospel Jesus or the apostles preached. Their message was that through Christ, the kingdom of heaven was coming *to be with us*; *Jesus* was the gift the Father was giving. To have Him is to have the reality of the resurrection, now and in the future. He was—and *is*—"the life."

If we are to dwell in the infinite gift of the new covenant, we cannot stay with the first-day Jesus, who merely fills our bellies with food—a temporal, finite satisfaction. We must move on to the second-day Jesus, who gives us Himself, even if it means leaving the blessings of the old covenant behind. We see this principle in the story of the rich, young ruler.

Now behold, one came and said to Him, "Good Teacher, what good thing shall I do that I may have eternal life?"

So He said to him, "Why do you call Me good? No one is good but One, [and] that is God. But if you want to enter into life, keep the commandments."

He said to Him, "Which ones?"

Jesus said, "You shall not murder," "You shall not commit adultery," "You shall not steal," "You shall not bear false witness," "Honor your father and your mother," and, "You shall love your neighbor as yourself."

The young man said to Him, "All these things I have kept from my youth. What do I still lack?"

Jesus said to him, "If you want to be perfect, go, sell what you have and give to the poor, and you will have treasure in heaven; and come, follow Me."

But when the young man heard that saying, he went away sorrowful, for he had great possessions.

Then Jesus said to His disciples, "Assuredly, I say to you that it is hard for a rich man to enter the kingdom of heaven. And again I say to you, it is easier for a camel to go through the eye of a needle than for a rich man to enter the kingdom of God."

When His disciples heard it, they were greatly astonished, saying, "Who then can be saved?"

But Jesus looked at them and said to them, "With men this is impossible, but with God all things are possible."
(MATTHEW 19:16–26)

On the surface, it may appear that Jesus presented the Law as the way to enter the kingdom of God. However, a deeper reading reveals that Christ was not just leading the young man to a commandment but to Himself. Jesus intentionally left out the first of the Ten Commandments: "You shall have no other gods before Me,"[6] and herein was the problem. With a simple request, Jesus laid bare the weakness of this wealthy man's heart.

Jesus said to him, "If you want to be perfect, go, sell what you have and give to the poor, and you will have treasure in heaven; and come, follow Me." (MATTHEW 19:21)

If this fellow was to follow Jesus into the kingdom of God, he would have to leave behind the old covenant definition of "the good life" for the new. His measure was money, and it had to become Christ. This is why the Lord commanded him to sell all he had and give to the poor, that he might have treasure in heaven. After all, he was not just giving up money; he was giving up one life for another—the finite for the eternal, the old covenant for the new. Most importantly, the Lord beckoned him to give up his false god for the *true* God of love and *seeing*. Money left him lacking, but Christ would give him the never-ending bread of heaven.

We should note that Jesus did not promise the young man more money if he gave to the poor; He did not say, "Give and God will give back many times what you give!" We often view giving as an investment, believing that our gift of money will ultimately deliver *more* money from God in return.

Giving has a much deeper meaning, however. Whenever we give, we lay aside the old definition of life, saying that neither money nor our possessions define us; they are not our completion. If they were, we could no more let them go than perish ourselves. But because Christ is all of these things to us, we have the freedom to give—*giving is worship*. Giving is the product of a love relationship with God.

Though there are times when God may give more to us than we give, this is only a secondary blessing. *God* is our reward when we give; *He* is the heavenly treasure. If that young man had let go of his money, he would have gained Christ as his life and discovered what he was lacking. However, he loved his old definition of life more than the life Jesus offered, so he walked away grieved.

When the people strayed in the Old Testament, they returned to their covenant—the Law—to realign with God and His blessings. But the story of the rich young ruler reveals that repentance in the new covenant finds a deeper meaning than right or wrong. *We stray when we wander away from grace.* Our lives also get out of order when we love the finite more than the infinite, opening ourselves to other masters who enslave us and leave our spirits empty.

Matthew 6, chapter 33, shows us the proper order of life: "But seek first the kingdom of God and His righteousness, and all these things shall be added to you." Rest assured, God knows the things we need, but *Christ* remains at the top of the list.

From a finite perspective, we often believe in rewards—property, possessions, wealth, status, even basics like food and water—more than we believe in God; we believe physical bread is more important than the bread of life. In chapter 11, we talked about knowing your mountain (Mount Sinai versus Mount Zion) and understanding that the new covenant is based on grace rather than works. In the same way, knowing our covenantal blessing helps us relate to and walk with the Lord. If we asked the Old Testament people of God what God wanted to give them more than anything, they would probably say the Promised Land—the great blessing of the old covenant. It meant *everything* to God's people, as it was part of their very identity. To lose the land to the Gentiles was to lose themselves, which is why the sermons in the book of Deuteronomy were so important.

In Jesus's day, the Jews were convinced that the land was God's plan for them and wanted their Messiah to give it back. Indeed, the land was their life, but Jesus came to give them something far greater: Jesus Himself was—and *is*—the new covenant dwelling, and He beckoned His beloved to come abide *in Him.*[7] No longer the people's measure, the land, which was a shadow, gave way to substance, and *having Christ* was to be alive and prosperous. Many misunderstood what Jesus wanted to give, however, rejecting God and the infinite in the process.

We must not make the same mistake in our day. A saying we hear often is that God has a wonderful plan for our lives. We quote Jeremiah 29:11: "For I know the thoughts that I think toward you," says the Lord, "thoughts of peace and not of evil, to give you a future and a hope." Though Jeremiah wrote this long ago, it is still true—as long as we understand its new covenant context.

How often have each of us said, "If God loved me, He would [fill in the blank]"? Such thoughts come from a heart that is fighting God in defense of a mirage. And if we never arrive at the Promised Land we signed up for, we might conclude that God does not deliver.

The life that finds completion in Christ is the truly accomplished life—the fulfillment of God's plan; when God thinks of His plan for our lives, *He thinks of Jesus.* And we must think of the same, for only then does our wrestling with God cease. Only then do we truly *see.* We come to understand that when we have God's gift, *we already have all things.*

In John, chapter 14, Jesus boldly proclaimed that He is the life—the truth on which all else depends. Every other definition of life, no matter how noble, is secondary. Fortunately, when we surrender our hearts to God's purpose, it is *freedom*, not slavery; *gain*, not loss. To be at peace with the Lord, we must let go of our definition of abundant life and embrace His. We must lose what was our life and find Christ instead.

The Prodigal

Then He said: "A certain man had two sons. And the younger of them said to his father, 'Father, give me the portion of goods that falls to me.'" So he divided to them his livelihood. And not many days after, the younger son gathered all together, journeyed to a far country, and there wasted his possessions with prodigal living. But when he had spent all, there arose a severe famine in that land, and he began to be in want. Then he went and joined himself to a citizen of that country, and he sent him into his fields to feed swine. And he would gladly have filled his stomach with the pods that the swine ate, and no one gave him anything.

But when he came to himself, he said, "How many of my father's hired servants have bread enough and to spare, and I perish with hunger! I will arise and go to my father, and will say to him, 'Father, I have sinned against heaven and before you, and I am no longer worthy to be called your son. Make me like one of your hired servants.'"

And he arose and came to his father. But when he was still a great way off, his father saw him and had compassion, and ran and fell on his neck and kissed him. And the son said to him, "Father, I have sinned against heaven and in your sight, and am no longer worthy to be called your son."

But the father said to his servants, "Bring out the best robe and put it on him, and put a ring on his hand and sandals on his feet. And bring the fatted calf here and kill it, and let us eat and be merry; for this my son was dead and is alive again; he was lost and is found." And they began to be merry.

Now his older son was in the field. And as he came and drew near to the house, he heard music and dancing. So he called one of the servants and asked what these things meant. And he said to him, "Your brother has come, and because he has received him safe and sound, your father has killed the fatted calf."

But he was angry and would not go in. Therefore his father came out and pleaded with him. So he answered and said to his father, "Lo, these many years I have been serving you; I never transgressed your commandment at any time; and yet you never gave me a young goat, that I might make merry with my friends. But as soon as this son of yours came, who has devoured your livelihood with harlots, you killed the fatted calf for him."

And he said to him, "Son, you are always with me, and all that I have is yours. It was right that we should make merry and be glad, for your brother was dead and is alive again, and was lost and is found." (LUKE 15:11–32)

We know this parable as the story of the prodigal son, but it is really the story of two sons. Both had relationship problems with their father, a parallel to humanity's relationship problems with God, but the illustration goes further than that: in them, we see the two greatest obstacles to living in the gift of Christ.

In an earlier chapter, we discussed the older brother, who thought his father's love was something he and his brother had to earn. Trying to make his father's love conditional rather than unconditional left him isolated from both his father *and* his brother. And contrary to what we might expect, at the end of the story, the younger, more sinful son rested securely in his father's house while the fate of the "good" son is left uncertain. Self-righteousness is a lonely path.

In this chapter, we turn to the younger son's story and two basic questions: Why did he leave home and why did his father let him go? The answers will help us understand our own journey into our heavenly Father's love.

The son's father was wealthy, so the young man did not want for anything. However, we might speculate that the father held the reigns too tightly or was too strict, which made the younger son want to escape. If this were so, however, would the father have given his son an early inheritance?

In that day and culture, the oldest son got a double portion of his father's wealth for an inheritance, and it was not uncommon for a father to give his sons their inheritance before he died—but there *were* strings attached. The father continued to live off the profits from the inheritance until he died; only then would his wealth pass fully to his sons. Giving an inheritance outright and then allowing a son to leave with it (and its profit-making potential) as the father in this parable did was very unusual.[1] Obviously, the prodigal's father gave his sons a great deal of freedom, even to make mistakes.

Another possibility is that the father did not love his sons enough. Unloved children find it easier to leave home, right? Yet the father's reaction at the end of the story contradicts this theory; he clearly wanted to be with his sons very much.

There can be only one explanation for the prodigal's straying: much like Eve in the Garden of Eden, he believed a lie.

Human beings are incomplete, like an empty cup that longs to be filled. God made us this way so we could find our completion in Him, but the fact that we are born lacking also opens us up to enticement—false fulfillment—from other sources.

The Tree of the Knowledge of Good and Evil tempted and captured Eve (with a little help from the serpent) even though it could not deliver the satisfaction it promised. The serpent portrayed the forbidden tree as a better choice than the Tree of Life, and who knows? Maybe it was more enticing than God's tree—could it have enticed Eve otherwise? If the Tree of Life had looked superior, certainly Eve would have refused its forbidden counterpart.

Folly often looks better than wisdom, its attractiveness blatant, external, and immediate. We can only see wisdom's beauty with the heart, and the difference between it and foolishness is the difference between love and lust: lust wears gaudy and enticing attire but only drains life; love sometimes appears unattractive but gives only life.

No doubt, the world out there appeared to be a better home to the prodigal son than his father's house, so he packed his bags and left. With a pocket full of money and the freedom to do whatever he wanted, he thought he was on the road to his dreams. In reality, he traveled the path to losing everything, but even his error had direction. As we shall see, because of the father's love, that same road was also the path back home.

Today, we citizens of the United States face the same temptations the prodigal did, only they are much bigger. We live in one of the most enticed nations ever, bombarded daily by advances that began in the twentieth century and have made it difficult for our hearts to stay at home in God's house ever since. In the span of 100 years, the United States has evolved faster than any civilization in history,[2] transitioning from a long-time agricultural society to an industrial society and then a computer-based society. And with each change came an enormous creation of wealth—an amount so large that it is difficult to grasp. To give some perspective, the people of the United States created more wealth in the twentieth century than the combined wealth of every civilization that existed before.[3] That means adding up *all the things* that *all of humanity* made in 10,000 years. And we beat that number in 100 years!

This unprecedented prosperity changed the soul of our country. An agriculturally-based society is a needs-based society. People hope for enough to meet their basic needs, and as long as they have a roof over their heads and food on the table, they consider themselves prosperous.

As the United States gained more things in the last century, its culture went from a needs-based society to a wants-based society. Now, having enough is of less import than having *more*, and in the case of food, quantity, variety, and speed trump quality and sustenance. Likewise, a roof over our heads is about bigger and better, with everything from air conditioning to a fast Internet connection. In Jesus's day, common folks had one or two sets of clothing—can you imagine? We have closets full, not to mention cars, boats, computers, cell phones, iPods, and big-screen TVs.[4]

Madison Avenue helped usher in these changes, using advertising to manufacture "need"—an appeal to the lust of the eyes—with "fresh and new!" and all the bells and whistles. For example, I drive an older model car, and it is a good car, rarely needing repairs and operating very reliably. I should be happy to have a car that has served me so well...but then I turn on my TV and watch a commercial presenting a new luxury car. *It looks so amazing* that I can almost smell the new car smell. It can talk to me and help me when I am lost. And look at all those cup holders! The fellow who owns that car looks happier than I, and everyone seems to think he is really *somebody*. I attract no attention when I drive my car, and it certainly does not make me smile every time I get in it.

Suddenly, I don't feel so blessed to have the vehicle I own. I look again at the car on TV, and I feel incomplete without it. Five minutes ago, I did not know it existed. Now, even if it means getting a huge loan, I feel like I have to have it.

Every time we turn on our TVs, we are likely to see a philosophy that is counter to the kingdom of God. It broadcasts materialism as the way to find fulfillment and points to stardom as the way to be somebody. In fact, we live in a star-struck culture. Celebrities attract attention with beauty and glamour that turn people's heads. And with this fame comes fortune, perpetuating the lavish life. Finances do not restrain celebrities like they do the rest of us. The images we see project the idea that to be complete we need to be good looking, rich, and famous. But are the stars really happier than anyone else, their every success and trauma plastered in the public eye? Keeping up appearances is a tyrannical ruler, too, masking an emptiness behind the scenes.

We often hear that the problem in our country is that we have forsaken our values. There is truth in this, but there is a deeper issue.

When the prodigal son in Jesus's story left home, he was not just leaving a set of principles; *he was leaving his father*. He was forsaking love for lust because the latter looked more appealing. He was fooled by the serpent just as Eve—and the United States—was fooled.

We would be wise not to let the philosophies of the world entice us. Like the Tree of the Knowledge of Good and Evil, they have the appearance of wisdom but most often lead to bondage. *We are free* when we do not need things to be full; *we find rest* when we do not need the world's attention to be important; *we avoid lust* when we do not require money or the approval of man to be complete. If the world—the external, the finite—does not give us life, it cannot take it away. With God's love as our gauge, our freedom knows no bounds.

Christians are not meant to copy the culture but to be subversive to it. Remember Jesus the rebellious winebibber who feasted with society's undesirables? We, too, are different because we have a one-of-a-kind treasure to share with the rest of the world—the treasure that comes from heaven. Too often, though, we preach a Jesus who is a twenty-first century American: follow Him and He will give you the American Dream. Such a message is *foreign* to the Gospel! Our good news is that God, through Christ, gave us Himself. *God* is the treasure—and the measure—of the kingdom of God, and when we live in our treasure, we shine! We celebrate! We partake in the infinite with Christ. Christ makes *everybody*, even the most lowly, a star.

When we become like the world, we have no power to change it. When our message centers on the world's treasure, we become irrelevant, just another voice among many. If we are to live our Christian mission, we must step out of bounds to show the world that human worth and completion are not found in beauty, fame, or possessions but in Christ. *This* is the wisdom of the Tree of Life, and it is the only wisdom that delivers. It is also the wisdom that the world is starving for. In Christ, *we gain a Voice*—a Voice that does not demand; It invites. It tells the children of the world that they can come home. Even now, their Father is running to embrace them.

So, why did the father in Jesus's story allow *his* son to leave home in the first place? He could have commanded the young man to stay and then offered him an extra reward for doing so. He could have tried fear, telling the young man that God punishes those who forsake their parents. But the wise father did neither.

Rewards and threats were the method of the old covenant, but blessings and curses did not keep God's son Israel at home anyway. The father in Jesus's parable knew that love is the only thing strong enough to keep the human heart from straying. He also knew that it would take a trip to ruin before the son could grasp the depth of his father's love. Sometimes the pigsty is the place from which we see most clearly.

Straying is often a part of the journey home. And the faster we run toward the darkness, the faster we reach the place where our deception *ends*. It is ironic that the sins of the world can be the perfect antidote for godlessness; when mired in the thick of them, our hearts turn toward home.

The journey of the wayward son was rife with ironies. He thought he left home for a feast, but he was really going to a famine. He thought he was headed for freedom, but he ended up being the slave of a Gentile. And his new master was cruel! What kind of a man would make a Jew feed pigs? Everyone knows Jews and pigs do not mix. Yet the prodigal was so low that even the unclean food that the unclean pigs were eating looked inviting to him.

This is an awesome picture of what happens when we seek completion in anything other than Christ. The Tree of the Knowledge of Good and Evil is a pigsty in disguise, and the serpent is a master of illusions, making that which is evil look good and that which is good look evil. He makes the path of lust appear to be the way to freedom and satisfaction. And he makes the way of love look like it only leads to loss. Temporal and limited (finite), the Tree of the Knowledge of Good and Evil can only look better than the Tree of Life for so long. When we come to our senses and see this tree's true nature, the Tree of Life looks more stunning than we could have ever imagined.

Coming to a place of seeing can be a tough road to travel, but God is with us every step of the way. Even when we fight against him, He fights *for us*. In the book of Acts, when Paul encountered the Lord on the road to Damascus, Christ said to the future apostle, "I am Jesus, whom you are persecuting. It is hard for you to kick against the goads."[5] In Jesus's time, a goad was a long metal pole with a pointed end that people used to direct oxen. And because the driver—like Jesus—was so far from the end of the device, trying to kick against it was pointless.[6]

Such is our wrestling against love. Even when love lets us go, we cannot outrun our destiny. God will be there, pushing us on, until we reach the end of the road and have to turn around to face Him.

Similarly, the wayward son—at his lowest and at the end of the line—decided to return home, and we can imagine what was going on inside him as he approached his father's house. It was probably a mixture of relief and dread—relief because he finally escaped famine and his cruel Gentile master, and dread because he had to face his father.

To reveal our vulnerabilities before another gives this person great power: he can either curse us by heaping more shame and condemnation upon us, or he can give us the gift of worth, forever changing us. In other words, he can give us what we deserve or he can give us *the opposite* of what we deserve. Which did the prodigal's father give?

No doubt, the prodigal son could not believe his eyes as his father *ran* to great him. Running was something servants did—rulers would not lower themselves is such a way! But this *one* did. He wanted to hug his son so much that he did not care what anybody thought.

Overcome with emotion, the father embraced and kissed and welcomed his son. He also ignored the young man's offer to become a hired servant and called instead for the best robe, some sandals, and a ring for his son's finger (a gesture for honored sons). When the son was expecting shame, the father gave him honor. When the son thought he deserved a rebuke, the father declared it time for a celebration. The father gave the son the opposite of what the young man deserved, and he did so lavishly, without a second thought.

Some say unconditional love can only lead to more sin, but this story illustrates *its power*. Do you think the son ever left home again? He came to obedience through *love*, not fear or a bribe, and it turned him into a true son. Such is the love of our Father in Heaven as well. Who could ever stand against it?

We sometimes view repentance as returning to a commandment, making promises to God that we will never do this or that again. We believe that what the Lord wants most is for us to change our behavior when the reality is much simpler: God's greatest desire is for us to *come home*. This is the essence of repentance—coming home to the Father who loves us—and unless we *let our Father give us the opposite of what we deserve*, we will always stray toward worldly things that fall short on *their* promises. The only cure for such temptations is finding completion in true love.

Once we see God as our home, we will want to stay; this is the revelation of a lifetime. It is the one God weaves into everything— even the Gentile's pigsty—to give us. And sometimes it takes a great deal of pain—a journey—to make us ready to see it. Once we come to our senses, however, the revelation is huge! Our prize is God and His prize is us. *We* are the ones He pursues even when He lets us go.

Worship

When we talk about worship, we usually speak of what it looks like. And we have seen just about *all* forms of worship at Thorncrown Chapel! We have had dynamic services where people danced in the aisles and shouted loud praises to God. Trumpets blared, people sang impromptu songs inspired by the moment, and some shook like the Quakers of old.

We have also seen worshippers on the opposite end of the spectrum. One day, a large group of Amish[1] came to a service. Most denominations cherish the back seats in the sanctuary, but not the Amish; they went directly to the front rows. There they sat, men with their long beards and women with their covered heads, and all dressed in plain, unadorned black clothing. To the Amish, even buttons are proud. I am normally a very conservative dresser, but that day, as I stood before them, I felt like I was wearing a glow-in-the-dark tie with a sequined jacket.

I am used to some sort of response when I preach and can usually tell if people are interested or not. This group of Amish gave me no clues—they sat motionless the whole time. Even the small children were amazingly still. I thought they must hate what they are seeing, or that or they were so scared they could not move.

To my surprise, when the service was over, they grew very animated and told us how much they enjoyed everything. I learned that stillness before God is the Amish way of worshipping; what I was seeing was merely their tradition. They were worshipping God as they did back home, which was quite a compliment.

So, what *should* worship look like? With so many different ways of praising God, this question may be impossible to answer, and perhaps we should not try. There is one question we should ask when we ponder worship, however, and that is, "What is worship?" As we consider this mystery, worship's form becomes less and less important. Worship is an expression of a love relationship with God that can be as unique as the person expressing it. The inward act is far more important than the outward form.

We should seek to accomplish worship every time we gather in the Lord's name. Yet to truly worship, we must know more about what we are trying to accomplish.

Worship happens when we receive God's love and love Him in return. And to help us understand what this means, God has given us illustrations in the scriptures. The Torah gave the Jews instructions on how to worship Yahweh, but no one has performed these ancient practices in almost 2000 years. They first require the Temple, and the Romans destroyed the last Jewish Temple in AD 70. These ancient practices still speak, however, as they are foreshadows of the new covenant relationship with God.

If we asked any Jew in the first century about worship, his answer would surprise us. In our day, we associate worship foremost with singing hymns and choruses to God. We tell God what we think of Him in song and call it worship. A first-century Jew would not think first of song but of sacrifice. Though the Jews of his era sang hymns as we do, sacrifice was the heart of worship in the ancient world. A visit to the Temple always coincided with shedding an animal's blood or burning an offering as a gift to God. Without some sort of offering or sacrifice, worship was not complete.

The Old Testament Temple rituals are far too complex to discuss in detail; Jewish priests had to study for years to master them. A lot depended on these fellows, as the Jews believed all of Israel could suffer the consequences if the priesthood did not get things right. The High Priest's responsibilities were especially vital because of his direct contact with the Holiest of Holies in the Temple and *Shekinah*; he *really* had to sweat the details. But as I said, we don't need to complicate matters by trying to interpret every little nuisance of the Jewish rituals. Let's step back instead and take a look at the big picture.[2] When we do so, we see an extraordinary illustration of new covenant worship and relationship with God.

The Jews gave three basic types of sacrifices, which portray the heart of worship. The first was the sin offering, and, as the name implies, this offering took care of or covered the people's sins depending on the variation used. Trespass offerings covered a single sin, while other kinds of offerings covered a whole individual and all of his or her shortcomings. At the great feasts, the priests gave sacrifices for the sins of all of Israel.

The High Priest presented the most solemn sacrifice on the Day of Atonement. It was the one day out of the year when a man could enter into the Holiest of Holies, and the whole nation depended on their High Priest to give an acceptable sacrifice. If he failed, they might lose their prosperity. The people nervously waited outside the veil as their High Priest entered into the most holy place to sprinkle the blood of a bull on the mercy seat, or throne of grace (as discussed in chapter 7). If the High Priest did not return from beyond the veil, the people knew Yahweh had not accepted their offering.

It is easy to see how the gift of Christ fulfilled the sin offering once and for all. He gave the ultimate sacrifice for all the world's sin for all of time. As the book of Hebrews says, the blood of bulls and goats could not remove sin; it could only cover transgressions.[3] Christ's sacrifice removed every offense *forever*.

He made Him who knew no sin to be sin for us, that we might become the righteousness of God in Him. (2 CORINTHIANS 5:21)

As we discussed in earlier in the book, Christ's sacrifice broke sin's hold on us so it can no longer keep us out of the Holiest of Holies. God tore the veil in two, and no one can put it back together.

But Jesus did more than put away sin; He gave us His righteousness. Now, when God sees us, He sees His own righteousness.

The Lord does not change His mind about who we are because doing so would deny Himself as well. He keeps a "righteousness consciousness" concerning us, but the problem resides with us human beings. *We* are the ones who change our minds about who we are. Though we have a righteousness consciousness at times, we can become very sin conscious when we fail. We feel far from God or abandoned by God completely.

At such times, we might think we need to do something to get God back, and we turn to religion. We try to feel sorry enough or humble enough to restore our relationship, performing religious deeds to appease a God who must be angry. Some even treat worship itself as a means to get near to the Lord: if we can just praise God enough, heaven will come down. However, worship is not a method for twisting God's arm. Such an attitude is actually *the opposite of worship*. Even if our focus is on worshipping well enough to please God, our focus is still on *ourselves* and *our performance*.

Worship is taking our eyes off ourselves and looking at Christ. It is not a show we put on for God; it is a change of consciousness from self to Christ. When we look away from what we have or have not done and look at Jesus, our righteousness consciousness returns. *It is He who defines us*, and through worship, we participate afresh in the fact that God has given Himself to us in His Son. We come to church not to give another sin offering but to live in the fact that Christ has already given the perfect sin offering. We come to live freely in what is finished.

Therefore, worship is a change of consciousness from sin to righteousness and from self to Christ. The goal of our music, singing, and other forms of praise is to look at Jesus—*worship is all about relationship with God*. It is part of living in the gift, and its form does not matter, for it is a matter of the heart. God comes to church to give Himself to us, and we are there to take the gift anew; worship is not for the "super spiritual." In fact, we need worship the most on our worst days, when all we can see is our failures.

And guess what? We do not turn our eyes upon Jesus alone. Even this we do together with the Lord. He helps us *see*—as if He opens our eyes and says, "Look at me!" And when we do, we know who we are, too.

Worship is about *togetherness*. It is the experience of union with Christ, and because we are one with Him, we are one with each other.

Therefore I urge you, brethren, by the mercies of God, to present your bodies a living and holy sacrifice, acceptable to God, which is your spiritual service of worship.
(ROMANS 12:1, NASV)[4]

The above passage might be a bit confusing to us in the twenty-first century—if Jesus was the ultimate sacrifice, why would God want us to give ourselves as a living sacrifice? Does He need another payment for sin?

As discussed earlier in this chapter, understanding Jewish Temple worship—in particular the three main sacrifices—solves this mystery. The second type of offering, a gift offering or burnt offering, had nothing to do with atonement. Like the sin offering, the gift offering's name reveals its nature. Gift offerings were the Jewish way of giving thanks to God, but an offering also meant the worshipper was giving himself to God. And the priests always burned the gift offering so that the giver could not get it back. The Jews also believed that the burnt offering produced an aroma that was very pleasing to the Lord.

God no longer needs or wants the sin offering. (Trying to add to what Christ has done is offensive.) Yet God still desires the gift offering, and the gift offering He wants is *us*. This, no doubt, is the living sacrifice Paul was talking about in Romans 12, which brings us to a second great aspect of worship: *worship is receiving God while giving ourselves to Him.* A worship service is an exchange of gifts where God gives and we respond by giving ourselves in return.

At one time or another, we all have said, "Lord, I give myself to you" in a beautiful and pure gesture of worship. But what are we doing when we give ourselves to God, and what does God do with His gift? Fortunately, we have only to look at the Old Testament gift offering to get a clue. In the old covenant, the priests, who represented God, burned the people's offerings so that they were permanently God's. In the New Testament, we see that "God is a consuming fire,"[5] and we are the offering God consumes.

When we begin to understand this, we see that worship is not something to take lightly. It is not for those who have only a casual interest in God. *It is for the lovers.* We often associate the term "love offering" with money, but according to Paul, we are the love offering that God cherishes.

In giving ourselves, we are also asking God to remove anything that keeps us from having Him. We see the fire of God at work in the Apostle Paul's life when he said that he "suffered the loss of all things, and count them as rubbish, that [he] might gain Christ."[6] His loss was his own righteousness, and his gain was the righteousness of Christ. One of God's great works in our lives is still to consume our self-righteousness that we might know the reality of our union with Christ.

God's fire has another equally important purpose in our lives.

And God spoke all these words, saying: "I am the Lord your God, who brought you out of the land of Egypt, out of the house of bondage.

"You shall have no other gods before Me.

"You shall not make for yourself a carved image—any likeness of anything that is in heaven above, or that is in the earth beneath, or that is in the water under the earth; you shall not bow down to them nor serve them. For I, the Lord your God, am a jealous God...." (EXODUS 20:1–5)

In the Old Testament, one of Israel's great transgressions was worshipping idols. We might think we have this commandment down since bowing down to graven images is not a part of our daily practice anymore. That was for ancient pagans. Yet idolatry has a deeper meaning that still extends to our day.

You've heard me say before that we human beings are like the empty cup that yearns to be filled: until we find something to complete us, we are never satisfied. Our journey toward completion is one of worship, and while it may sound strange, *everyone* has a god and everyone worships—even atheists. Our god is whatever we think will complete us, and we willingly give ourselves to our god with the hope that he/she/it is up to the task of making us whole.

The scriptures tell us that God desires our worship, but this does not mean that the Lord needs a bunch of people to tell Him how wonderful He is. Rather, *worship is a love issue.* This is why the Lord called the Israelites adulterers when they went after false gods. God desires to give Himself to us and for us to give ourselves to Him—so that we might *be one.* It is in this relationship that we find completion.

False gods are the things we give ourselves to instead of God; they are the things we allow to take the Lord's place. We worship what is most important to us, as our hearts dwell on what we worship. If we have something in our lives that we desire more than God, we probably have an idol. We may not sing about it on Sundays or pray to it every night, but we still have a false god that has seduced us. James expresses the Lord's heart on this matter in his Epistle

Where do wars and fights come from among you? Do they not come from your desires for pleasure that war in your members? You lust and do not have. You murder and covet and cannot obtain. You fight and war. Yet you do not have because you do not ask. You ask and do not receive, because you ask amiss, that you may spend it on your pleasures. Adulterers and adulteresses! Do you not know that friendship with the world is enmity with God? Whoever therefore wants to be a friend of the world makes himself an enemy of God. Or do you think that the Scripture says in vain, "The Spirit who dwells in us yearns jealously"? (JAMES 4:1–5)

At times, we are so disillusioned that we go so far as to *ask God* to give us our idol. We pray for something other than God to give us worth and make our lives complete. Our false god has blinded us to the point that we ask the Lord for something to take His place! This is like a wife asking her husband to provide another husband. James tells us that this provokes God, and it is no wonder that He does not answer.

Once something has captured our heart, it is hard to let it go. Yet this is part of loving God fully. Sometimes we have to let go of what we love to find *true love*. (No one said worship is easy.) Giving the gift offering often means laying our first love on the altar to be consumed; giving our first love to God is giving ourselves to God. Anyone who has ever been to the terrible and holy place of the gift offering knows this is true. It is the place where *we lose all to love so that we might gain love.*

In the first book of Kings, God's people had an idol problem. Ahab was the king of Judah at this time, and though we might not know his name, we all remember his wife, Jezebel. She turned an entire nation away from God to worship the false god Baal. In response, the Lord sent a drought that lasted several years. Yet the people did not turn from their folly.

Now, before we condemn these ancient Judeans or start feeling good about our superiority, we must realize that we have *all* done the same thing. We have all given our heart to another love, and then the drought came. Even so, we persisted or found yet another love to take the place of God in our lives.

We see God's mercy even in the drought, tirelessly guiding His people to help them *see*. However, when the famine has served its purpose, it is time for the rain. And it comes through an act of worship.

Elijah was the prophet of God in those days, and he challenged Ahab to one of the most unusual contests in the Bible. The prophet told Ahab to bring 450 prophets of Baal and 400 prophets of Asherah (Baal's wife) for a showdown at Mount Carmel. There, they would decide who the *true* God was. It was 850 to one! And Ahab must have like those odds, because he agreed.

The children of Israel came along with Ahab and his prophets to watch the show—imagine the spectacle as one man faced down an entire nation! Then Elijah challenged Baal to a test: both he and the pagan prophets would present a sacrifice, and the god who sent fire from heaven to consume the offering was the real Lord of all.

Elijah, being the polite prophet that he was, gave Baal's fellows the first try. They put on quite a show, crying out and dancing for their god. Elijah speculated that Baal was occupied and said that they should yell louder and try harder. They did, even cutting themselves to gain their god's attention. But Baal never showed up.

Then it was Elijah's turn. It was the time of the evening offering— gift offering to God. The prophet erected an altar of twelve stones, prepared the sacrifice (a bull), then dug a trench around the altar and filled it with water three times.

At this point in the story, we are knee-deep in symbolism, with the twelve stones representing the twelve tribes of Israel and the bull representing Christ.[7] Israel itself was the gift offering, but the offering was thoroughly wet—as if in resistance to the fire. Even so, Elijah merely asked God to send the fire from heaven, and it came, consuming not only the offering but also the altar and the water surrounding it.

This is a beautiful picture of the human heart when we give the gift offering to God. Often, we come to the Lord with love for another god that we cannot resist. Our heart resists letting go of that which we love most, and all we can do is present ourselves without pretense before God. As long as our altar—our intention—is sound, He'll send the fire from heaven.

There is a sense of togetherness even in the gift offering. It is something accomplished together with God: we present, God consumes. He may take away that which we love entirely, or He may give it back. But even if He does give it back, it will no longer be ours. The gift offering is an act of excruciating loss, but it is also a moment of infinite gain. Because after the fire comes the rain.

When the Judeans saw what God had done, they fell on their faces and cried out, "The Lord, He is God! The Lord, He is God!"[8]—a vital revelation. For there is more to our relationship than just finding out that God is in charge; *it is finding out that God is the one who completes us.* Only those who give the gift offering get to behold such glory—a glory that puts us on our faces. The altar is the place where God takes the veil from our eyes and we see who He is.

Once Elijah had dispatched the false prophets, he went to the top of Mount Carmel to pray. And when the time was right, the Lord sent the rain, a symbol of His presence come down from heaven to touch the Earth. In fact, the rain mingling with the Earth is all about *togetherness*, which brings us to Israel's third great sacrifice, the peace offering.

The peace offering was not really a sacrifice but an act to symbolize the entering into and enjoyment of what the sin and gift offerings accomplished. It was always the last of the three types of offerings, and it was the most joyous of all. In many respects, it was like having a celebratory meal with God. And depending on the type of peace offering, either the priests or the worshippers literally ate what was offered.

Back in that day (as in ours), eating together was an intimate occasion. Families and friends shared meals together, people made business deals and forged alliances over meals, and festive events such as weddings always included at least one meal. In all scenarios, sharing a meal signified *togetherness.*

Likewise, the peace offering was a celebration of oneness with God. It was a "sit down" with the Lord and remains a primary goal of worship today. *We gather together* to receive God's gift afresh; *we gather together* to present ourselves to God as a living sacrifice; and *we gather together* in recognition that we *arrived together*, not only with God but with each other. The peace offering is not about giving or receiving; it is about enjoying God's company and the fact that *He enjoys ours*—a mutual sharing of one's innermost being, in love and unafraid.

— 17 —

Intimacy with God

Even though the scriptures clearly say that God is near and intimately involved in our lives, His closeness is still hard for us to grasp. He is so otherworldly and holy that we might think He cannot relate to us and we cannot relate to Him.

We humans have enough trouble relating to each other, let alone God. For example, the rich usually do not mix with the poor, "sinners" do not often associate with the "saints," and people with conflicting political views rarely stick together. Sometimes, even the slightest differences keep us apart, making us most comfortable around people who are like us.

What if God is the same way? As David said in the Psalms, "Lord, what is man, that You take knowledge of him? Or the son of man, that You are mindful of him?"[1] How can the infinite and the finite mix— the perfect be with ones who are so flawed? We hear the illustration that God is so far above us that comparing ourselves to Him is like comparing ants to humans. Why would God want to associate with ants?

Maybe this is why the Lord is always telling us to do what He would do. If we are a little more like Him, He might be more comfortable with us. Yet at times, telling us to behave like God seems like telling an ant to be human. It does not seem very fair.

To be honest, we are not sure we want to be with God all that much either. We sing "What a friend we have in Jesus" on Sunday, but in secret, we wonder if He is a friend we really want around. We think He is so religious, and we believe He does not like many of the things we do. Maybe we can visit Him on Sundays and Wednesdays, but we are not sure we want to be with Him *every* minute of *every* day.

Considering the alternative, we certainly want to go to heaven! And God has some pretty good blessings to share with us here on Earth. God is worth following for these things, but is God worth following just for God?

We never vocalize such concerns, but our actions betray our hearts. Usually, we spend far more time asking God for His blessings than we do asking to know the Lord. Likewise, we talk far more about working for God than possessing God. Maybe we should try to look at things from God's perspective: if we had a loved one who wanted our gifts or employment *more* than they wanted us, how would we feel?

Relationship issues more times than not come from misunderstandings. We have incomplete information, so we draw incorrect conclusions. This is why communication is the lifeblood of a strong relationship, and our relationship with the Lord is no different. If we think God does not want us around, we have some bad information. In fact, the scriptures reveal that He wants to be with us more than we want to be with Him. To the Lord, the thought of not having us near is *unbearable*. If this was not so, Christ never would have gone to the cross.

Similarly, if we think God is someone we would not want to be around, we do not have all the facts. We have heard the expression "to know him is to love him," and there is nobody this applies more to than the Lord. As we get to know Him, not having Him present becomes unthinkable. And if we do not want Jesus *more than anything*, we do not fully know who He is.

God tried to explain Himself in multiple ways throughout His relationship with humanity but ultimately sent His Son to perform the task.[2] Originally, God gave us the creation to help us see what He is like, but we did not get it. Then He gave us His Law and worked wonders for us, but we still did not understand. Finally, He sent Jesus to do the talking—almost as if the Father looked at the Son and said, "*You* go tell them!"

Christ became one of us so we could see what God is like. Christ's actions, the people He loved, and the people He came against showed God's heart. Then, through the showdown and gift of the cross, God screamed at the top of His lungs, "*This* is who I am!"

As if that was not enough, God followed His Son's coming with the words of the apostles, giving us teachings and wondrous images to help us to further understand. And God's pictures speak loudly of what He desires for us and from us. We see images such as the vine and the branches, the temple of the Holy Spirit, the body of Christ, and the bride of Christ. If we think God is far away or only visits us on occasion, these images quickly dispel such ideas. They reveal that God is nearer and more intimately involved in our lives than we could possibly imagine.

We tend to think the differences between God and us make such wonderful closeness impossible. God is infinite, we are finite, and the latter, certainly, cannot conceive of the former. However, this is not the hindrance to intimacy with God we might think. On the contrary, because God is infinite, *He can be closer to us than any human being.* God is able to know us completely and love us completely in a way that *no one else* can.

Full disclosure and unwavering love are two great measures of a close relationship; for intimacy to occur, we must be able to reveal ourselves to another and still be loved. No human being is able to accomplish this like God, who fully knows us and fully loves us. Period. Human love may stop when we see each other's weaknesses and failures, which is why we so diligently hide our shortcomings. Fear makes us masters of disguise, but God's love does not stop. He knows not only our actions but our thoughts, and He still loves us relentlessly. The Lord's infinite capacity to both know *and* love makes Him the best companion we could ever hope for.

Even better, it is the Lord's greatest desire to be closer than any other in our lives. He wants the infinite and the finite to be joined together. We first see this in the Old Testament house of God, where the Jews believed the Holiest of Holies in the Temple was the place where heaven touched Earth. In the New Testament, God boldly revealed His heart when He said that *we are His temple.*[3] *We* are the house God has fashioned for Himself.

The Apostle Paul used other astonishing imagery to help us understand what God wants most. One of the most powerful is the marriage illustration.

> *For we are members of His body, of His flesh and of His bones. "For this reason a man shall leave his father and mother and be joined to his wife, and the two shall become one flesh." This is a great mystery, but I speak concerning Christ and the church.* (EPHESIANS 5:30–32)

We have many weddings at Thorncrown Chapel, and I try to help our couples understand what they are doing on their wedding day. When they stand at the altar, they are not just making a promise to stay together no matter what; they are giving the greatest gift a human being can give to another—the gift of self. The bride and groom give themselves to each other in a way unequaled in any other human relationship. With the mutual gift of self, something mysterious and wonderful happens: the two become one.

The marriage relationship clearly points to our relationship with the Lord. For example, on your wedding day, all your spouse owns becomes yours and vice versa, but this is not the reason you got married. If it were, it would cheapen the relationship. Likewise, accepting the Lord is more than receiving mandates on how to live or answering a call to service. How many of us married our spouse solely because we wanted to work for him or her or because we could not wait to be faithful to one person? Such things are qualities of a good relationship, but they are not its essence.

When we receive Christ, *we receive a Person*, not a mere commandment or call to service. He gives us the gift of Himself, we give ourselves to Him, and…the two become one. Marriage is about union, and our relationship with the Lord is no different. Things like possessions and behavior are products of union, but union can only happen when God is a gift.

Our relationship with God is the best relationship we have. Yet the way we often present Him stifles intimacy and turns the Lord into someone who is the furthest from us rather than the closest.

Straight from the Old Testament, much of our teaching leads us to believe that what God wants most is for us to behave correctly. We conclude that because our lives have so many troubles, God is obviously disappointed in us. If we can become someone God would want to be around, we'll be someone He wants to bless. Such messages are then followed by a formula to get the job done—anything from moral living to having faith.

This idea destroys intimacy, setting up a performance-based relationship with God in which our behavior dictates whether God is with us or not. Even faith can be a performance we put on for God when we are told God turns His back if we do not have enough of it. Ironically, *true faith is seeing that God never turns His back*.

Intimacy can only occur in an environment where no performance is necessary. If we have to earn our place with God, we open the door to fear of rejection. Closeness with the Lord grows and flourishes in the rich fertile ground of love, not the sterile ground of fear.

Fear is the enemy of intimacy. If we have to measure up, we will hide from God whenever we fail Him. Recall what Adam did when he disobeyed, hiding himself in the Garden. If we do not hide ourselves from God, we will not feel that God is hiding from us. Being able to share our shortcomings is an integral part of a close relationship. But for this to be possible, love must first banish fear.

> *There is no fear in love; but perfect love casts out fear, because fear involves torment. But he who fears has not been made perfect in love. We love Him because He first loved us."*
> (1 JOHN 4:18–19)

Jesus came to reveal the love of God once again. Before He came, it was as if God wore a covering; the veil in the Holiest of Holies was God's shroud. In reality, it was *Adam's choice* that veiled God—*He* chose the Tree of the Knowledge of Good and Evil over the Tree of Life. He looked at himself rather than at God, and, in doing so, *he became blind.* When self became his righteousness, he could no longer see the love of God. *He became trapped* in a framework of trying to be someone God could accept.

Jesus achieved His revelation by tearing apart the covering humanity's sin had put on Him. And He began by accepting people no one else would accept and by loving lavishly those no one else would love. When we think of Jesus being perfect, we think of Him never doing anything wrong. But this is a limiting view on His perfection. Jesus *loved perfectly.* The world had never seen such love! In light of it, the veil could not compete—especially at the cross. When Jesus breathed His last, God tore the veil surrounding the Holiest of Holies from top to bottom. *Jesus humbled Himself in a way that offends the blind but compels the seeing to worship*, suffering unimaginable rejection so we could know unimaginable closeness to the Father.

This perspective clarifies the maturity of which John speaks in his Epistle. We often view Christian maturity as getting closer and closer to God, but true growth occurs as Christ removes the coverings we have put on God—coverings He banished long ago at a place called Calvary. We come to see what Paul called the "width and length and depth and height" of the love of Christ.[4] Becoming mature is the process of love's triumph over fear.

Thinking of love as a ruler may be difficult for us, but love is— literally—King. Fear, the weaker ruler, can bring us to exhibit certain behaviors but only to control us against our will. It says, "obey or else." Interestingly, fear and its accompanying performance-based relationship then lead *us* to try to control God through good works, having faith, and other religious deeds. We try to use our behavior to get God to do what *we* want.

Fortunately, unlike fear, love is a ruler to which we willingly bow. In the presence of infinite grace, all resistance melts away, one gift begets another, and we give ourselves to the one who loves us *no matter what.* When God says "I love you" to the human heart through Christ, we become love's willing participant—as God already is. This is the way relationship with God is meant to work—as two beings who give of themselves out of love and not control.

Part of knowing how much God loves us is knowing how much He sincerely wants us. We might think God loves us because it is His duty as Love the King—that because of our inferiority, loving us is His sacrifice, not His pleasure. I have even heard people say that the Lord loves us, but He really doesn't *like* us. If we are to know intimacy with God, however, we must know *we are infinitely welcome in His presence*. In fact, the Lord yearns for our fellowship.

We saw in the book of James that God is a "jealous" god—a description one would not expect to hear in regard to someone who does not earnestly desire us. In fact, this jealous nature alone shows how much God wants us because *no one* is capable of wanting us more than God infinitely does.

This concept is difficult for us to grasp, as jealousy is not typically a redeeming quality. However, what God selflessly did to gain us shows that we are His prize, His ultimate love. Perhaps during our high school or college days we had a boyfriend or girlfriend who broke up with us and ended up with someone else soon after. Devastating as it was, what if our ex had made a bad decision? What if his or her new love turned out to be a very big mistake—how would we feel then? If we are honest, we would admit that it probably makes us feel pretty good. Our former love was getting what he or she deserved.

The Bible often portrays God as a jilted lover but in a marriage context. We left Him for another lover called the world, and it did not work out for us; leaving God was a very bad choice. Amazingly, the Lord did not turn His back, leaving us with "what we deserved." He came to get us instead.

Who among us would willingly serve the one who rejected us? Who would go after him or her *knowing more rejection awaited*? Beyond even that, who would *die* for this person in order to take on the consequences he or she deserved? God would, and He did so through Christ and the cross. If we look to Calvary, there can be no doubt of God's passion for us.

We are told to make the Lord our greatest love, but we cannot do so until we see that we are God's greatest love as well. No reward, no matter how great, can make us love God more than anything. Fear cannot accomplish it either. *It is love that makes us love.* Once we can conceive of God's unending love for us, we cannot help but love Him in return.

> *No longer do I call you servants, for a servant does not know what his master is doing; but I have called you friends, for all things that I heard from My Father I have made known to you.*
> (JOHN 15:15)

"The Lord works in mysterious ways"—we've all heard the expression, which translates as: God will not tell, so do not ask. Jesus's words in John 15:15 contradict this overused cliché, however. Being friends means sharing intimate secrets with each other, and it means being able to ask why and expect an answer.

There are times in our lives when things do not make sense. Perhaps God seems strangely absent, or it may look like He is withholding the things we need. He may even take away what we have for no apparent reason—*but God does not operate without intention.* If we will let Him, God, our friend and confidant, will take us up, as if on a high mountain, so we can see the big picture. We will see that He is always there, especially when we think He is not, and we will see that anything "lost" is taken away to make room for something greater.

God is not afraid of the question "Why?"—He expects us to ask it. And He is delighted when we do, for it is an opportunity to reveal the gift to us.

Years ago, I suffered from an unusual digestive disorder that would not go away and found myself asking why. I awoke each morning wondering what my bowels were going to do to me that day, and at times it was so bad that I could not preach or do my job. I prayed and prayed that God would make it stop, and all sorts of other people prayed, too. For two years, I held on to my faith that God would deliver me, and for two years, nothing happened. Finally, I ran out of faith.

I still remember the conversation I had with the Lord. I told God I was so tired and disappointed that I could not believe Him anymore. And you would think the Lord's response for a faithless preacher would come in the form of a lightning bolt! Instead, it was as if the Lord took me up to that high place and let me see. He showed me that *faith is not holding on to God but seeing that God holds on to us—even when we let go of Him.* He allowed me to reach the end of my faith so I could live in *His* faithfulness. God was giving me something all along, but I could not see it. He was giving me Himself, and who can argue with love? When it showed itself, all I could do was apologize and let it in.

I got well soon after that, but I gained far more than my health. I got a taste of God's gift, which heals both the body *and* the soul. That day, my relationship with the Lord changed, but it would not have been possible if I had not run out of my faith. There, at the end of my faithfulness, I began to live in grace.

One of the great journeys in life is self-discovery. That is why statements such as "I am what I am" and "it's what I do" are such powerful proclamations. But getting to know who we are is not something we do alone. Self-discovery is a journey we take with God. And as much as intimacy with God is getting to know who God is, it also getting to know ourselves.

Each of our lives is a unique picture of God's glory, and each is a picture of Jesus. By divine design, your one-of-a-kind picture does not look like mine, yet we still tend to think that everyone's life should be a copy of ours. Evangelists think everybody should be an evangelist; teachers think all people should share their zeal for teaching. I do not know how many people have come up to me and told me what *I* should be doing! What they were really saying, however, is that my picture of Jesus should look just like theirs, and such thoughts, though innocent, are an offense to the Master Artist. *He* is infinitely creative. That is why every picture is so special and as priceless as the next. To think any less is to devalue not only ourselves but God Himself.

The Lord knows us better than we know ourselves, and it is His delight to share you, His creation, with the world. In the movie *Chariots of Fire*, missionary Eric Liddell said, "When I run, I feel God's pleasure." Likewise, when we find God's pleasure, we find our own pleasure—our own joyful calling. God has given each of us something to do *together* with Him.

Patricia Taylor, our music minister at Thorncrown Chapel, says she feels closest to God when she sings. Do I feel closest to God when *I* sing? Have you ever heard me sing???

Because I am a preacher, people might think I feel closest to God when I preach. However, this is not the case. I am an explorer, and I am happiest when I am seeing something about God that I have never seen before. That is who am I, and that is what I do. Yet if I try to do these things alone—without God—I end up empty. Being who we are and doing what we do is something we do *together* with the Lord. And getting to know ourselves is part of living in God's grand gift.

As we walk with the Lord, He reveals the mysteries of our lives, but *He* remains as the greatest revelation we'll ever discover. While our delight is to reveal ourselves to God without fear, God's delight is to reveal Himself—His infinite love—to us in the finite. And when the Lord shows His glory to us, it is not to prove His superiority or to put us in our place; it is *love in action*. When God shows Himself, it is always a presentation of the gift, and it is always to raise us up to where He is, so we can participate in it. When God says, "this is who I am," He also says, "...and all I am is yours."

Getting to know God is the process of finding out that He is not who we thought He was; He's infinitely *better*. This is why the prayer to know the Lord may be the most important prayer we pray. God's answer will transform us and what we see when we look at the world. When we ask the Lord to change our lives, He will answer by revealing Himself to us, thereby changing our lives *forever*.

Jesus opened the eyes of many a blind man, yet that was only to point to His greater task. He came to open the eyes of humanity so we could see just how very much God loves us. When we began our walk with God, the Lord's love was shrouded by our own self-righteousness, and we were blinded by the fool's gold of other loves. Now, Christ touches our eyes *and we see*. *We see* that God is our prize and *we see* that we are His. And *we see*, from His high place, that this has always been so...and it will *always* be so.

— 18 —

Seeing Further

Then Jesus spoke to them again, saying, "I am the light of the world. He who follows Me shall not walk in darkness, but have the light of life." (JOHN 8:12)

Darkness and light, seeing and blindness are constant themes in the New Testament. Even though darkness and light are about seeing or not seeing, we tend to think of these concepts in terms of good and evil. We tie the light to the good guys and the darkness to the bad guys.

The media and popular culture heavily reinforce this interpretation. For instance, in the movies, there is often an antagonist who represents the darkness. The actor who plays him has the job of making us dislike his character, and he does so by doing bad things. The actor who plays the protagonist represents Hollywood's idea of good and light. His job is to make us identify with and care about him so that we're on *his* side in the clash between good and evil that invariably follows. If we leave feeling satisfied that the bad guy got properly punished and the good guy got his just reward, we say the actors did their job well.

Jesus did not fit into popular culture in His day, and He would have the same problem in our day. His definitions always went against the grain. For one, He did not define light and darkness according to the deeds of humanity. To Christ, light was *a Person—He* was (and is) the light of the world. When we see the glory of who Christ is and what He has done, we walk in the light; when we do not, we walk in darkness. And if you recall, we can only see His light when we *look away from ourselves and our deeds*—good or evil—and look at Jesus.

This idea goes back to the beginning and the Garden of Eden. The essence of the Tree of the Knowledge of Good and Evil was less about evil and more about *separation*. To partake of this tree was to exalt the self over God—to take one's eyes off of Christ and gaze at oneself instead. This is *spiritual blindness*. When Adam lost the Tree of Life, he lost the light. Darkness fell, and it began to rule humanity.

Humanity began to define everything from the context of separation. New, self-centered definitions arose—designations that excluded God and changed the very definition of good and evil. Formerly, the Tree of Life was our connection to God, our personal measure. With Adam's choice, good and evil became centered on humanity's deeds. *What we did* defined whether we were good or bad, removing God's hand—His love—from the equation and imposing limits on the boundaries of our worth.

Additionally, we began to define things like riches and beauty by looking at ourselves rather than the Lord. In such a mindset, those who have less *are* less and those who have more *are* more. You cannot have the beautiful if you do not have the ugly; and in order to know the rich, there have to be the poor. Separation from God extended to our relationships with each other as well, creating a steadfast "us" and "them" mentality. We defined who was in (good) and who was out (bad) by looking at ourselves.

Unfortunately, even with the gift of Christ, we still look to the self to determine our personal worth and whether or not our life is good. When we ponder our lives, we usually think of the things we have or do not have, the things we have achieved or failed to achieve, or even how much pain we have known or not known. These conclusions, when based on comparisons between ourselves and others, are flawed from the start, only focusing on finite portions of the big picture. From God's perspective, this is living life in the shadows.

And there are other temporal things that cloud our thoughts about the state of our lives. If we are in a sour mood or sick, our lives can seem glum. Even the weather can affect our outlook on life. Usually, how we view our own life spills over onto our worldview. People who think the world is a rotten place usually think their own lives are rotten and unfair, too.

We can go even further by adding genetics to the equation. Some people are naturally "up" and some are naturally negative. This, when combined with our past experiences, also influences how we define our lives. To top it all off, we have a constant diet of TV news telling us about the awful things happening all the time.[1] No wonder we have a constantly changing opinion on ourselves, our lives, and the world.

Yet when we look away from ourselves and look at Christ, *everything changes*. We begin to look at our lives and the lives of others from the context of union rather than separation. Seeing becomes an action we share with God, eliminating the incorrect conclusions we reach when we go at it alone. Christ is the 24/7 channel that enables us to see who God is, who we are, and who our neighbor is *forever*. Looking at Him allows us to see that our lives are very good, no matter what.

This is the essence of faith. Looking at our world apart from Christ leads to disbelief. *Faith comes from togetherness with God.* It is seeing in the light of Jesus and what He has done—the gift He has given.

Such thoughts lead to questions—questions that may conclude that God made us blind on purpose to make us dependent on Him. Why would He do such a thing?

We have only to look to the gift to find the answer. God's great desire is to give Himself to us. He wants us to view the world through His eyes and partake of the mind of Christ. We were not made for aloneness in any capacity, even in seeing, which is why the self-centered road perpetuates its limits and isolation. When we take God's gift, the light shines on love's open road and an existence where *all things are possible.* We see God, our world, and who we truly are for the first time.

Now, since Christ has come and removed the veil, any walls between God and us are of our own making. They exist only in our own minds and not in the mind of God. When we gaze at Christ, the God who is hidden or only visits occasionally fades away, and we behold the God who is always near. Likewise, the God who only gives us morsels of conditional affection disappears, and we see the God who is lavish in His love. *The greatest repentance, therefore, is changing our thinking to match God's.* The Apostle Paul wrote about this to the church in Rome.

> *Do not be conformed to this world, but be transformed by the renewing of your mind, that you may prove what is that good and acceptable and perfect will of God.* (ROMANS 12:2)

The mind of the world is separation and has been so ever since Adam and Eve partook of the forbidden fruit. The mind of Christ is union, and finding it will transform us. Paul exhorted the church to renew its mind, though he could have just as easily said, "Open your eyes! Look at Jesus, and you will experience God's perfect will." The Lord's perfect will is our togetherness with Christ. His will for us is the Tree of Life.

In John's Gospel, he identified himself as the disciple "whom Jesus loved."[2] Some say this is because John always seemed to be closer to the Lord than the other disciples, though Jesus clearly loved His other disciples (He loves *all* of us!). I think there is some truth to John's statement, however—a truth that goes much deeper. John *grew to identify himself* as someone Christ loved.

As we gaze upon Christ, we gain a similar revelation. We look at ourselves and say, "I am not who I thought I was. I am someone God loves—someone not on the outskirts but close to Jesus's side." This new identity leads to a new relationship with the Lord in which He is our destination, not a far-off vacation or weekend visit. His presence becomes our home—the place we never leave.

A life where we only see who we are and what we have done is a walk in darkness, but the light of Christ illuminates like none other. With Him, *everything becomes a sight to behold.*

If we can look in the mirror and see "someone God loves," great peace and joy will be ours for eternity. We'll come home because the quest to become someone God wants to be near will end; God, our Father, is happiest alongside His creation! And our life as a treasured disciple will begin. If we do not have such a vision of ourselves, however, we may need a bigger glimpse of Jesus.

Likewise, seeing Christ dictates what we see when we look at our neighbor. Jesus saw something entirely different than a Pharisee did when He looked at a tax collector. If we have contempt for our neighbor, our eyes are on ourselves again rather than on Christ. But one look in the opposite direction—*just one*—and we will see that even the worst sinner carries the title "beloved." It is a simple choice: Look at your neighbors through the eyes of the law and see the world as a hopeless, forsaken place. Or look at the world through the eyes of grace and witness a place of infinite possibilities—one whose future is in the sure grasp of God rather than the feeble hand of humanity. Is there *really* a choice to be made?

God tore down the walls between Him and us and, in doing so, removed the walls that separated us from our neighbor. If we put the walls back up for any reason, we have put on our blinders and stepped into spiritual darkness again. Such separations do not and cannot exist in the heart of God, and we should not allow them to exist in our heart either.

The light of God's gift also shines on the circumstances of our lives—*when* we're willing to look in that direction. If we live by the Tree of the Knowledge of Good and Evil, however, we decide if our lives are going well by weighing our bad circumstances against our good circumstances, comparing our lives to others' lives on the scale of happiness, and/or stacking up our good and bad deeds to determine whether our lives are acceptable to God.

When we look at Christ, detached views like these give way to a new definition of the good life, and it is *not* measured by our circumstances but by the gift. What is the good life? It is a life filled with Christ. Even with loss and disappointment, God is giving Himself. *He is always giving Christ*—sometimes even more so in the bad times. How, then, can we have ingratitude in our hearts? How can we ask, "Why me?" If we view ourselves as one to be pitied, our eyes are on the self rather than Christ. *When God opens our eyes to the gift, our lives, no matter their circumstances, become a wonder.* (You didn't know the "Why me?" question had an answer, did you?)

When we see God's purpose is the gift, we begin to see His hand in places and times we never have before—our seemingly random lives now appear miraculously planned! And accepting the life God intends is part of accepting the gift; ingratitude only multiplies our blindness. With God's vision, we can comprehend Paul's great statement to the Thessalonians: "In everything, give thanks; for this is the will of God in Christ Jesus for you."[3]

We often ask the Lord to change our lives, and it is typically a request to either give us something or take something away. In reality, the best thing to ask for is *the ability to see as He does*. Rather than seeing something unsatisfactory or lacking, God observes a place where the finite and the infinite create a wondrous union. Great wealth, worldly beauty, popularity, or even perfect circumstances fail to compare! The divinely inspired dance between our Creator and us is taking place always and in all things. We have only to (you guessed it) *open our eyes* to this joy, the essence of a good life.

Therefore, since we have such hope, we use great boldness of speech—unlike Moses, who put a veil over his face so that the children of Israel could not look steadily at the end of what was passing away. But their minds were blinded. For until this day the same veil remains unlifted in the reading of the Old Testament, because the veil is taken away in Christ. But even to this day, when Moses is read, a veil lies on their heart. Nevertheless when one turns to the Lord, the veil is taken away. Now the Lord is the Spirit; and where the Spirit of the Lord is, there is liberty. But we all, with unveiled face, beholding as in a mirror the glory of the Lord, are being transformed into the same image from glory to glory, just as by the Spirit of the Lord. (2 CORINTHIANS 3:12–18)

In the Old Testament, Moses asked to see God, and the Lord took him, put him in the cleft of a rock, and gave him a partial glimpse of His glory. We might think that Moses, being *Moses*, could ask such a thing. Yet Paul tells us in 2 Corinthians that we all are beholding the glory of God "with unveiled face," and seeing God's glory changes us.

The glory of the old covenant was a fading glory because it was based upon the Law. And such is the glory of our efforts to get God to be with us. Throughout history, there have been what we call "moves of God," which are usually preceded by extreme human efforts. People repent of the evil in their lives or try to move God with their many prayers. Like the glory on the face of Moses, the splendor of such revivals always fades, and many times, disastrously.

The New Testament suggests a new paradigm: *God* has moved. He did so long ago when He tore the veil in the Holiest of Holies. He moved right next to us and has been there ever since, His glory as steadfast as the cross. We just need to see Him.

Some people longingly wish for a return to the Garden of Eden. But their vision of the Garden is either a world without pain or a world where everyone gets along—behaves properly. If Adam and Eve had only passed by the forbidden fruit, we would live in a world without sickness, suffering, and perhaps even physical death.

Utopian as it is, such a view of the Garden is still flawed. Again, it puts our focus on ourselves rather than Christ, leaving us in a paradigm where the world was once a place God could love. Now, it is a place He cannot wait to destroy! It redefines God's purpose from perfect union to perfection itself and actually *robs* humanity of the gift. Humanity's purpose and quest is for perfect union, plain and simple. God and us together—now *that's* a perfect world.

Jesus said the kingdom of God is within us,[4] and the Garden God wants for humanity is in the same place. It is the place where God gives the gift of Himself and we give ourselves in return. It is not a perfect utopia but *perfect love*. The Garden of Eden is a place of the heart.

If you think about it, a flawless world is not the best place for humanity to find its destiny. Imperfection and trouble create the best environment for us to grow into the meaning of love and grace, thus knowing union with Christ. It is the place from which we can most clearly see the gift. How can a perfect person behold the majesty of grace? She will never be able to fall on her knees and worship in the presence of unconditional love because she has no reason to receive it. Our world is exactly the way it is supposed to be: the perfect place for us to come to understand our union with our Creator.

This does not mean, however, that we should not try to make the Earth a better place; "home improvements" provide the perfect platform for building union with God. If, when we look out the window, we say, "God hates this place," the world will always be hopeless and ugly. On the other hand, if we look out the window and can say, "beloved," we will see hope and beauty in the most terrible places. There is no better toolkit than infinite love.

One has to imagine that this is what Jesus saw when He walked among the worst sinners, the downtrodden, and the demon possessed. He saw beloved Israel and a fertile, perfect place for germinating God's gift. If He had seen anything else, we would still be without hope.

But let us *not* hope for a return to utopia; let us realize instead that *paradise is here now*. We have only to turn our eyes to Christ to see it.

Paradise is living in the gift of God.

Thanks be to God for His indescribable gift!
(2 CORINTHIANS 9:15)

Endnotes

Introduction
1. Matthew 22:37, Mark 12:30.
2. 1 John 4:16.
3. Romans 6:14.
4. Exodus 33:12–23.

Chapter 1: From the Beginning
1. John 10:10.
2. In this book, I often reference the historical context of the New Testament. Understanding the minds of the people who wrote the scriptures enriches the Bible dramatically, and the same is true for any literature. For example, suppose we pick up a copy of part one of Tolkien's *The Lord of the Rings*, and we randomly pick out a sentence that talks about Frodo, Sam, Pippin, and Merry leaving the shire. We could dissect every word in that sentence, defining each one carefully while figuring out certain things like the speed they were walking and other small details. And after all our work, we might say, "Big deal, they left home." However, if we attempted to get a bigger picture by looking at the whole story, we would reach a different conclusion. When we understood what a Hobbit was and the great troubles of the day, we might say something like, "They left the shire! Wow!"
3. John 14:6.
4. The Romans generally used rods to inflict punishment, and the Jews used whips. And Torah forbade a sentence any more than forty lashes (Deuteronomy 25:1–3). Whenever I need a quick glimpse of the setting of a passage such as this one, I reach for two sources: the New International Version of the *Archaeological Study Bible: An Illustrated Walk Through Biblical History*, edited by Walter C. Kaiser, Jr., and Duane Garrett (Zondervan, 2006), and the *Holman Bible Dictionary* (Holman Bible Publishers, 1991). Both are excellent.

5. 2 Corinthians 11:22–29.

6. Philippians 3:8.

7. Luke 18:10–14.

8. 1 John 4:7.

9. Exodus 3:13–14.

10. Judges 6:22–24.

Chapter 2: The Two Trees

1. John 14:6.

2. Genesis 2:16–17, 3:4–5.

3. Ephesians 2:5.

4. Luke 15:22–24.

5. Exodus 26:31.

6. Genesis 3:24.

7. Genesis 3:19.

8. John 17:3.

9. Romans 3:23.

Chapter 3: The Return of the Gift

1. Deuteronomy 28.

2. Matthew 19:23–26.

3. *The Dictionary of Jesus and the Gospels*, edited by Joel B. Green, Scot McKnight, and I. Howard Marshall (IVP Academic, 1992), has an excellent section on the Jewish idea of clean and unclean. For a more detailed study of this subject, I recommend *The New Testament World: Insights from Cultural Anthropology*, by Bruce J. Malina (Westminster John Knox Press, 2001).

4. In the Old Testament, we read that the nation of Israel split into two nations: Judah, which was made up of the tribes of Judah and Benjamin, was to the south; and Israel, which was made up of the other ten tribes, was to the north. The Judeans kept their Hebrew bloodline intact while those of Israel did not. Many Judeans, therefore, thought God favored them more than other Jews. In Philippians, chapter 3, when speaking of his own righteousness, Paul wrote that he was of the tribe of Benjamin. In other words, he was of one of the tribes that got it right.

5. Acts 10:28.

6. *The Passion of the Western Mind: Understanding the Ideas That Have Shaped Our Western World*, by Richard Tarnas (Ballantine Books, 1993), and *The New Testament World: Insights from Cultural Anthropology*, by Bruce J. Malina (Westminster John Knox Press, 2001), are both excellent resources on this subject.

7. Luke 2:8–15.

8. In their book *The Jesus Movement: A Social History of Its First Century* (Fortress Press, 2001), Ekkehard W. Stegemann and Wolfgang Stegemann give a very detailed analysis of the social and economic conditions of the first-century world. They describe in detail the effect high taxes were having on the common man.

9. Luke 19:1–10.

10. Leviticus 6:4–5.

11. Luke 19:9.

12. *The Message and the Kingdom: How Jesus and Paul Ignited a Revolution and Transformed the Ancient World*, by Richard A. Horsley and Neil Asher Silberman (Augsburg Fortress Publishers, 2002), contains a wealth of information about the Pharisees, Sadducees, and the Essenes.

13. Deuteronomy 28:21–22 and Exodus 34:7.

14. *The Dictionary of Jesus and the Gospels*, edited by Joel B. Green, Scot McKnight, and I. Howard Marshall (IVP Academic, 1992).

15. No study of the historical Jesus is complete without the works of N. T. Wright, whose insights are brilliant. For an introduction to Wright's work, I would recommend *The Challenge of Jesus: Rediscovering Who Jesus Was and Is* (IVP Books, 2011). If you want to take a deeper look, try his more scholarly work *Jesus and the Victory of God* (*Christian Origins and the Question of God*, vol. 2 [Augsburg Fortress Press, 1997]).

16. *Bandits, Prophets, and Messiahs: Popular Movements in the Time of Jesus*, by Richard A. Horsley with John S. Hanson (Trinity Press International, 1999), is an invaluable tool for understanding the tensions between the Romans and the Jews.

17. *The Jesus Movement: A Social History of Its First Century*, by Ekkehard W. Stegemann and Wolfgang Stegemann (Fortress Press, 2001).

18. The writings of Josephus describe the history of first-century Palestine in great detail. This prolific writer also gave us an account of Jewish history from Adam to the Jewish–Roman wars. His works are not easy reading, but fortunately there is a condensed version: *Josephus: The Essential Works*, translated by Paul L. Maier (Kregel Academic & Professional, 1995).

19. When it comes to understanding the Jewish Temple, I turn to *The Temple: Its Ministry and Services*, by Alfred Edersheim (Hendrickson Publishers, 1995).

20. Mark 5:1–17.

Chapter 4: Participation in the Gift

1. For an excellent study on the Sermon on the Mount and the kingdom of God, I would recommend *The Divine Conspiracy: Rediscovering Our Hidden Life in God*, by Dallas Willard (HarperOne, 1998).

2. Luke 14:15–24 and Matthew 22:1–14. People called Jesus a glutton and a winebibber—a reputation had to have come from somewhere. Most likely,

when Jesus came to a person's house, it was not a solemn occasion but a joyous celebration of the kingdom of God. And much food and drink were shared by all.

3. Ephesians 1:22–23.

4. *Bandits, Prophets, and Messiahs: Popular Movements in the Time of Jesus*, by Richard A. Horsley with John S. Hanson (Trinity Press International, 1999).

5. Even Peter could not accept a crucified Messiah (Matthew 16:21–23).

6. In their book, *Recovering the Scandal of the Cross: Atonement in New Testament and Contemporary Contexts* (IVP Academic, 2000), Joel B. Green and Mark D. Baker use contemporary Japanese society to help us understand the honor- / shame-based society of Jesus's day. It is a fascinating study. *The New Testament World: Insights from Cultural Anthropology*, by Bruce J. Malina (Westminster John Knox Press, 2001), also has good material on the subject.

7. Luke 6:28, Romans 12:14–21.

Chapter 5: Opposition to the Gift

1. Matthew 12:45, 16:4.

2. N. T. Wright's books *Jesus and the Victory of God* (*Christian Origins and the Question of God*, vol. 2 [Augsburg Fortress Press, 1997]) and *The New Testament and the People of God* (*Christian Origins and the Question of God*, vol. 1 [Augsburg Fortress Press, 1992]) contain in-depth information about the various groups and factions in first century Palestine, as does Richard A. Horsley and Neil Asher Silberman's *The Message and the Kingdom: How Jesus and Paul Ignited a Revolution and Transformed the Ancient World* (Augsburg Fortress Press, 2002).

3. Matthew 11:19. See also chapter 4, endnote 2.

4. John 7:20, 8:48, 52 and John 10:20–21.

5. Luke 20:25.

6. Matthew 23.

7. Luke 15:11–32.

8. *Josephus: The Essential Works*, translated by Paul L. Maier (Kregel Academic & Professional, 1995).

9. Richard A. Horsley and Neil Asher Silberman's *The Message and the Kingdom: How Jesus and Paul Ignited a Revolution and Transformed the Ancient World* (Augsburg Fortress Publishers, 2002) is an excellent resource on the Herods and the Caesars.

10. *Josephus: The Essential Works*, translated by Paul L. Maier (Kregel Academic & Professional, 1995).

11. Ibid.

12. You can read a great lecture on Rome and the early church by N. T. Wright called "Paul's Gospel and Caesar's Empire" at ntwrightpage.com/Wright_Paul_Caesar_Empire.pdf.

13. *The Days of Vengeance: An Exposition of the Book of Revelation*, by David Chilton (Dominion Press, 2006).

14. Ephesians 2:1–7.

Chapter 6: The Kingdom of God Is Bigger Than Being Right

1. It was Luther who refused to shake Zwingli's hand, and it is said that Zwingli wept openly because of it. Lest we pat Zwingli on the back too much, he continued to oppose Luther and later refused to join forces with the Lutherans. Ted Byfield has a wonderful series of books on the history of the church called *The Christians: Their First Two Thousand Years*. Volume 9, called *A Century of Giants, AD 1500 to 1600* (Christian History Project, Inc., 2010), has outstanding material on the Reformation. The book *The Unquenchable Flame: Discovering the Heart of the Reformation*, by Michael Reeves (B&H Academic, 2010), is also very good.

2. Proverbs 23:7.

3. For a whirlwind tour of the growth of the Western mind, *The Passion of the Western Mind: Understanding the Ideas That Have Shaped Our World View*, by Richard Tarnas (Ballantine Books, 1993), is exceptional.

4. For an enlightening study on Paul's body terminology, I recommend *The Body: A Study in Pauline Theology*, by John A. T. Robinson (Bimillenial Press, 2002).

5. To catch a mind-blowing glimpse of the cosmos, pick up a copy of *The Elegant Universe: Superstrings, Hidden Dimensions, and the Quest for the Ultimate Theory*, by Brian Greene (W. W. Norton & Company, 2010).

6. *New Light on the Difficult Words of Jesus: Insights from His Jewish Context*, by David Bivin (En-Gedi Research Center, 2005), gives wonderful insights of the Jewish Rabbis of the first century.

7. *Holman Bible Dictionary* (Holman Bible Publishers, 1991).

Chapter 7: The Cross

1. Penal substitution is not the only way the church has understood the atonement through the centuries. There have been several models that were popular in different time periods, and we could spend hours debating which way of presenting the cross is best. However, I wonder if such debates are warranted.

Joel B. Green and Mark D. Baker have a very interesting chapter (chapter 6) about foreign missionaries in Japan in their book *Recovering the Scandal of the Cross: Atonement in New Testament and Contemporary Contexts* (IVP Academic, 2000). When Western missionaries brought the Gospel to Japan, they presented it using our concept of penal substitution, and the Japanese did not respond. They could not relate because their system of justice is based on honor and shame as opposed to guilt and punishment. It was only when the missionaries used the framework of the Japanese culture to describe redemption that the people responded. Paul did the same thing, using various images to present the Gospel in a way that suited the audience/region.

So, which atonement model is indeed the best? I would say the answer varies from person to person and from culture to culture. Another book I found helpful on this subject is *Christus Victor: An Historical Study of the Three Main Types of* the Idea of the Atonement, by Gustaf Aulén, translated by A. G. Herbert (Wipf & Stock Publishers, 2003).

2. 1 Corinthians 5:7.

3. Hebrews 9:26.

4. Matthew 27:46, Mark 15:34.

5. Galatians 2:20.

6. Ephesians 2:1–7.

7. Recovering the Scandal of the Cross: Atonement in New Testament and Contemporary Contexts, by Joel B. Green and Mark D. Baker (IVP Academic, 2000).

8. Hebrews 12:2.

9. 2 Corinthians 5:21.

10. 1 John 3:2–3.

11. Romans 6:1–11.

Chapter 8: The Meaning of the Rent Veil

1. Jesus and the Victory of God, by N. T. Wright (Christian Origins and the Question of God, vol. 2 [Augsburg Fortress Press, 1997]).

2. The New Testament and the People of God, by N. T. Wright (Christian Origins and the Question of God, vol. 1 [Augsburg Fortress Press, 1992]).

3. The Temples That Jerusalem Forgot, by Ernest L. Martin (Academy for Scriptural Knowledge, 1994).

4. The Temple: Its Ministry and Services, by Alfred Edersheim (Hendrickson Publishers, 1995).

5. Matthew 21:13, Mark 11:17, and Luke 19:46.

6. The Message and the Kingdom: How Jesus and Paul Ignited a Revolution and Transformed the Ancient World, by Richard A. Horsley and Neil Asher Silberman (Augsburg Fortress Press, 2002).

7. Gregg Cantelmo has an excellent and well-documented article called "How Jesus Ministered to Women." You can find it at http://bible.org/article/how-jesus-ministered-women.

8. Luke 16:13.

9. In John, chapter 4, we read the story of the woman at the well. At the end of the story (John 4:27), Jesus's disciples "marveled that He talked to a woman." This story is extraordinary because this woman—rather than a man—became Christ's chief witness in Samaria. Moreover, the revelation that Jesus was the Messiah came first to a woman, something the Jews considered completely unacceptable.

10. Numbers 18:1–7. By the first century, such distinctions were often ignored. The election of the High Priest, especially, had become largely political.

11. 1 Peter 2:5.

12. Ephesians 2:19–22.

13. Matthew 24:1–2.

14. *The Veil Is Torn,* AD *30 to* AD *70: Pentecost to the Destruction of Jerusalem,* edited by Ted Byfield (*The Christians Their First Two Thousand Years,* vol.1 [Christian History Project, Inc., 2003]).

Chapter 9: Paul and the Law

1. Acts 16:1–3.

2. Galatians 5:12.

3. 1 Corinthians 5:7.

4. Hosea 6:6.

5. *Exposition of Chapter 7:1–8:4: The Law: Its Functions and Limits,* by D. Martyn Lloyd-Jones, (*Romans,* vol. 6 [Banner of Truth Trust, 1973]). D. Martyn Lloyd-Jones's commentary in this series has some remarkable insights on the function of the Law.

6. Romans 7:24. Some take this verse to mean that the physical body is evil. However, Paul most likely is talking about something corporate rather than our individual physical bodies. The body of sin is set against the body of Christ, and both terms have a covenantal context. If you can find *The Body: A Study in Pauline Theology,* by John A. T. Robinson (Bimillenial Press, 2002), it offers a very helpful voice on this difficult subject.

7. Matthew 16:24–27, Mark 8:34–38, Luke 9:23–26.

8. We must avoid the temptation to be anti-Semitic when we read the New Testament. The conflict of that day was between those who embraced God's gift and those who opposed it, and the Jews, who were God's chosen, were at the heart of this struggle. They were the ones through whom God would give the gift back to the world. Unfortunately, there were those of Israel who thought being chosen meant they were better than others. On the contrary, the purpose of their unique calling was to bring this unique calling to the whole world.

Chapter 10: Dead to the Law?

1. Colossians 2:14.

2. Acts 16:1–3, Acts 21:17–26.

3. Acts 9:4.

Chapter 11: Know Your Mountain

1. *Archaeological Study Bible: An Illustrated Walk Through Biblical History,* edited by Walter C. Kaiser, Jr., and Duane Garrett (New International Version; Zondervan, 2006).

Chapter 12: Our Wilderness Journey

1. John 15:15.
2. Genesis 37–50, 1 Samuel 16–31.
3. Matthew 5:3.
4. Rob Bell has an excellent presentation on Jesus and his disciples called "Covered in the Dust of Your Rabbi." It is available for viewing at various places on the Internet.
5. Galatians 6:11.
6. 2 Corinthians 1:8.
7. If you are interested in the work of Fay Jones, I recommend the book *Fay Jones*, by Robert Adams Ivy, Jr. (American Institute of Architects Press, 1992). Copies of this book are scarce, however, so here are a few alternate resources: *Outside the Pale: Architecture of Fay Jones*, Department of Arkansas Heritage (University of Arkansas Press, 1999); *Sacred Spaces: The Architecture of Fay Jones* (DVD), produced by Larry Foley and Dale Carpenter (University of Arkansas Press, 2010).
8. John 13:8.

Chapter 13: Seeing

1. Revelation 1:18.
2. I found this passage in a book called *Ancient-Future Faith: Rethinking Evangelicalism for a Postmodern World*, by Robert E. Webber (Baker Academic, 1999). It contains wonderful insights on worship and the early church.
3. Rob Bell gives some of the background surrounding Caesarea Philippi in his book *Velvet Elvis: Repainting the Christian Faith* (Zondervan, 2006), which I highly recommend.
4. 2 Corinthians 3:12–18.
5. For a good snapshot of the historical context of the book of Acts, see Frank Viola's *The Untold Story of the New Testament Church: An Extraordinary Guide to Understanding the New Testament* (Destiny Image Publishers, 2005).
6. 2 Corinthians 1:8.
7. This information was taken from an essay by N. T. Wright entitled "Reading Paul in the Context of Empire: Roman Imperialism, Pauline Resistance, and Contemporary Implications," available at http://miketodd.typepad.com/files/paul-the-politics-of-empire.pdf.
8. Romans 12:2.

Chapter 14: The Life

1. Job 42:12–17.
2. Deuteronomy 28:1–14.

3. John 14:6.

4. *Archaeological Study Bible: An Illustrated Walk Through Biblical History,* edited by Walter C. Kaiser, Jr., and Duane Garrett (New International Version; Zondervan, 2006).

5. John 10:10.

6. Deuteronomy 5:7.

7. John 15:4.

Chapter 15: The Prodigal

1. *Archaeological Study Bible: An Illustrated Walk Through Biblical History,* edited by Walter C. Kaiser, Jr., and Duane Garrett (New International Version; Zondervan, 2006).

2. For a fascinating look at the changes that occurred in United States during the twentieth century, track down a copy of William Van Dusen Wishard's *Between Two Ages: The 21st Century and the Crisis of Meaning* (Xlibris, 2000). It is hard to find but is well worth the effort.

3. Ibid.

4. It is possible that the American Dream reached its highest glory in the twentieth century and is now fading. Unfortunately, the fuel for much of the explosive growth in the United States was debt, and that debt is catching up with us now. Our children and their children may someday conclude that the American Dream was an illusion—one that they have to pay for and reap no benefit from.

5. Acts 9:5.

6. *Holman Bible Dictionary* (Holman Bible Publishers, 1991).

Chapter 16: Worship

1. You might think I am mistaken in saying a group of Amish folks came to Thorncrown Chapel since they do not use any modern forms of transportation. However, the Amish do, on occasion, use public transportation like trains and buses. The next question would be about *why* they wanted to visit us. And I can only say that Thorncrown's reputation has reached some pretty amazing places. One fellow brought me a magazine from Japan that featured the chapel on the cover. Perhaps news of Thorncrown's craftsmanship reached the Amish community as well and prompted a visit. I will never know why they came that day, but I will always cherish the fact that they did.

2. If you really want to study the details, I recommend *The Temple: Its Ministry and Services,* by Alfred Edersheim (Hendrickson Publishers, 1995).

3. See Hebrews, chapters 9 and 10.

4. I chose to use the New American Standard Version for this passage because it brings out the idea of worship. Other translations end this verse by saying that presenting ourselves to God is our "reasonable service." While this implies a service of worship, I believe the NASV translation is clearer on the matter.

5. Hebrews 12:29.

6. Philippians 3:8.

7. That the bull represented Christ shows us that even the gift offering is something we give through Christ. On the cross, He became the fulfillment of the gift offering; as He was consumed by God, we were consumed along with Him. When we give ourselves afresh to the Lord, we are actively participating in the fact that we belong to God through Christ. Therefore, the gift offering is as much an act of faith as it is an act of love.

8: 1 Kings 18:39.

Chapter 17: Intimacy with God

1. Psalms 144:3.

2. John 1:18.

3. 1 Corinthians 3:16, 6:19; Ephesians 2:19–22.

4. Ephesians 3:17–19.

Chapter 18: Seeing Further

1. The fact that the media gives us a diet consisting almost entirely of bad news is not a conspiracy to make us all depressed; it is economics. There is a saying among journalists—"bad news sells"—and it is true. Something in our human nature draws us to news about negative events, and those who present the news are well aware of this.

2. John 19:26; 20:2; 21:7, 20.

3. 1 Thessalonians 5:18.

4. Luke 17:21.

Index

About
Thorncrown Chapel

Nestled in a wooded setting, Thorncrown Chapel rises forty-eight feet into the Ozark sky in Eureka Springs, Arkansas. This magnificent wooden structure contains 425 windows and over 6,000 square feet of glass, and it rests on more than 100 tons of native stone and colored flagstone. The chapel's simplicity and majestic beauty make it what critics have called "one of the finest religious spaces of modern times."

Thorncrown Chapel was the dream of Jim Reed, a native of Pine Bluff, Arkansas. In 1971, Jim purchased the land to build his retirement home, but so many people stopped by to admire his view of the beautiful Ozark hills that he began to consider a different use for the property. Instead of fencing the people out, Jim decided to invite them in. He thought he and his wife, Dell, should build a glass chapel in the woods to inspire their visitors. It took faith and persistence for Jim to complete his dream, but Thorncrown Chapel finally opened to the public the summer of 1980. And it has received over six million visitors since.

Recognized internationally for its architectural lineage, Thorncrown stands apart as one of the exceptional buildings designed by world-renowned architect E. Fay Jones. Jones was born in Pine Bluff, Arkansas, in 1921, and he studied his craft at the University of Arkansas; Rice University; the University of Oklahoma; and finally, at the Taliesin Fellowship, under his mentor Frank Lloyd Wright.

Jones's awards include the 1981 American Institute of Architecture National Honor Award for Thorncrown Chapel and the AIA Gold Medal (1990). Thorncrown was listed fourth on the AIA's top ten buildings of the 20th century, and before his death in 2004, Mr. Jones was recognized as one of the top ten living architects of the twentieth century.

The inspiration for Thorncrown Chapel was Sainte Chappelle, Paris's light-filled gothic chapel, and Jones affectionately labeled Thorncrown's style as "Ozark Gothic." The chapel is made with all organic materials to fit its natural setting, with the only steel in the structure forming a diamond-shaped pattern in its wooden trusses. The building's native flagstone floor and rock walls give the feeling that the chapel has always been part of its Ozark hillside.

In order to preserve Thorncrown's natural setting, Jones decided that no structural element could be larger than what two men could carry through the woods. The building materials are primarily pressure-treated pine 2 x 4s, 2 x 6s, and 2 x 12s, and the larger elements of the building such as the trusses were assembled on the floor and raised into place.

Light, shadows, and reflections play a major role in Thorncrown's ambience. Because of the chapel's elaborate trusses and the surrounding trees, constantly changing patterns of light and shadows appear throughout the day. At night, reflections of its cross-shaped lights appear to surround the entire building. Consequently, Thorncrown never looks quite the same, its appearance changing every hour of every day and during the different seasons of the year.

Thorncrown Chapel is located a mile and a half west of Eureka Springs on Highway 62 West. It is open daily to the public from March through December, and on Sundays, the Thorncrown staff holds services for their guests. All are welcome to attend and hear the message of God's wonderful gift. Please visit www.thorncrown.com for more information.

Give the Gift of

God Is a Gift
Learning to Live in Grace

to Your Friends and Colleagues

Note: All proceeds from book sales will go to
Thorncrown Chapel, a nonprofit organization.

❏ **YES**, I want _____ copies of *God Is a Gift* at $14.99 each, plus $4.95
shipping. Canadian orders must be accompanied by a postal money
order in U.S. funds. Allow 15 days for delivery.

❏ **YES**, I am interested in having Doug Reed speak or give a seminar
to my church, association, school, or organization. Please send
information.

My check or money order for $_____ is enclosed.

Name _____

Organization _____

Address_____

City/State/Zip _____

Phone_____ E-mail _____

Please make your check payable to Thorncrown Chapel and return to:

Thorncrown Chapel
12968 Hwy. 62 West
Eureka Springs, AR 72632

Phone: 479-253-7401

www.godisagift.com

Made in the USA
Lexington, KY
16 April 2015